MOUNTAINS IN THE SEA
Table Mountain to Cape Point

'Over centuries the mountain has stood as a symbol of human capacity for hope and freedom, whether for the Khoikhoi tribes fighting colonial domination, for Indonesian and Malaysian slaves who for generations buried their leaders and holy men on its slopes, or for twentieth century political prisoners. It is ... a sacred and precious place ... To us on Robben Island, Table Mountain was a beacon of hope. It represented the mainland to which we knew we would one day return.'

– *Nelson Rolihlahla Mandela*
1998

SOUTH AFRICAN
NATIONAL PARKS

Produced for SA National Parks by

JOHN YELD and MARTINE BARKER

Text by John Yeld (*unless otherwise indicated*)
Design by Martine Barker

Photographs by Anton Pauw, John Yeld, Peter
Steyn, photographers of Independent
Newspapers (Cape) & Trace Images, George
Branch, Mike Fraser, Liz McMahon, Andrew
Jenkins, Callan Cohen, Charles Griffiths, Bill
Branch, Ukuvuka-Operation Firestop, Bruce
Sutherland of the City of Cape Town, Brenton
Geach, Dawid de Bruin, Hout Bay Museum,
Cape Archives, Fish Hoek Valley Museum, Chris
& Tilde Stuart, Melanie Gosling, René Navarro

Illustrations by Liz McMahon, reproduced by
courtesy of David Philip Publishers; Claire
Abbott, reproduced by courtesy of Hazel
Smithers and Struik Publishers; Mary Matham
Kidd, reproduced by courtesy of the Botanical
Society of South Africa; and Tobie Beele,
reproduced by courtesy of SA National Parks.

Cartography by Peter Slingsby

Maps reproduced under Government Printer's
Copyright Authority No. 11131,
dated 8 May 2003

First edition 2004
ISBN 0-620-31740-X

©Copyright 2004 SA National Parks

Published by SA National P
PO Bo
Constantia,

Printed by Pearl Print

MOUNTAINS IN THE SEA
Table Mountain to Cape Point

SOUTH AFRICAN
NATIONAL PARKS

AN INTERPRETIVE GUIDE TO THE
TABLE MOUNTAIN NATIONAL PARK

Sponsored by the French Global Environment Facility

HOW TO USE THIS GUIDE

The pages of this book are divided into History; Ecology; Out & About in the Park; Beyond the Park; and Maps and Contacts sections. Locate these in the Index or Contents pages and by colour tags on the outer edges of each page (see key below).

Examples of the things you will see in the Park and factual information about them.

Warnings of danger or places that you need good sense to manage safely

Practical information including phone numbers.

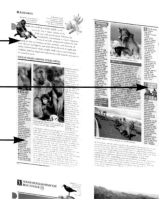

Details of what you can expect on walks in the Park such as times, distances and level of difficulty.

Maps of the Peninsula and details to help you find your way to the Park and around it when you go hiking.

Cross-references to related information in other sections indicated by symbol and page numbers such as ▲ 56/7

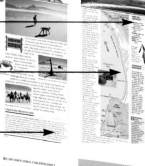

Colour-coded sections for easy reference (see key below)

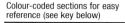

Tales and anecdotes: the Park is full of places where local folklore adds charm and colour

Historical information

Information boxes with details that tell you more about specific aspects of a subject.

REFERENCE for TRAIL MAPS

Roads, with Route number	M 62
Private Roads with public access	
Trails described in this book	1
Other footpaths	
Entry points; Parking	P
Picnic sites; Fires allowed	
Dogs allowed; Restaurants	
Signposts; Drinking Water	

The trail maps in this book are extracts from Peter Slingsby's **Cape Peninsula National Park Map Series**. Maps 1 to 5, reproduced here with permission. Use of these maps by hikers is recommended. Information from Baardskeerder cc's **Cape Peninsula – the map** is reproduced with permission of the publisher.

SECTION COLOUR CODES

○ History
● Ecology of the Park
● Out & About in the Park
● Beyond the Park
● Maps & Contacts

■ Every effort has been made to ensure that the information in this Guide is accurate and up to date. The publisher and the authors do not accept responsibility for any inaccuracies or changes that may have occurred. Visitors use the Park at their own risk and are strongly advised to read all safety warnings in this book and to obey all Park rules and regulations.

CONTENTS

■ GOING 'WILD' IN THE PARK

A Park for all, forever. That's the motto of this Park and careful thought has gone into putting real meaning into what could otherwise have been just an empty slogan. Among SANParks' many goals are two which are actually in conflict: making South Africa's national parks accessible to everyone, and generating sufficient income to meet management's conservation obligations. This Park pioneered the system which has now been introduced in all the other national parks and which potentially reconciles these two conflicting goals.

AFFORDABLE VISITS FOR ALL

CENTRAL TO SANPARKS' GOALS is the aim of affordable access, and this particular Park pioneered a scheme that has now been extended in a slightly modified form to all the other parks in the network. This was the introduction of the Go Green Card, which ensured that the four traditional pay areas on the Peninsula – Cape of Good Hope (Cape Point), Boulders, Silvermine and Oudekraal – remained affordable to South Africans in general and to Capetonians in particular.

Boulders Beach: Penguin viewing from the boardwalk.

Daily time check: The Noon Day Gun on Signal Hill.

The annual Go Green Card was an innovative scheme that allowed purchasers unlimited free entry to all four pay sections of the Park, as well as offering them substantial discounts and special offers at a range of other tourism facilities, including restaurants and, at times, the Table Mountain cableway.

In June 2003, SA National Parks adopted a similar but more sophisticated scheme involving the use of "smart cards" that contain a micro-chip similar to a credit card that can be swiped to effect transactions. This is the WILD Card scheme, introduced in partnership with the company Infinity. Holders of the WILD Card are exempted from a new, daily conservation fee now levied on all visitors to South Africa's 20 national parks in place of the old once-off entrance fee.

DEPENDING ON THE PARK being visited and the status of the visitor, the conservation fee ranges from R15 to R120 per person per day. WILD Card holders enter free. There are four pay areas in this Park where the annually recalculated daily conservation fee is levied: Cape Point, Boulders, Silvermine and Oudekraal. At the Cape Point section, this was R35 until 31 October 2004, irrespective of whether the visitor is a South African, a foreign visitor or a citizen of a Southern African Development Community (SADC) state. For adults, the fee at Boulders was R15; at Silvermine R10; and at Oudekraal R10 (2004). South Africans and SADC nationals who purchase a WILD Card will get a range of preferential entry rates, special offers and other benefits at restaurants and museums, and discounts for air travel and car hire. In January 2004, the cost of the WILD Card for South African nationals to visit one park for one year was R95 for an individual, R175 for a couple, and R195 for a family. The respective costs for cards valid for all parks were R120, R225 and R245. SADC members pay the same rates for a card valid for six months. Overseas visitors can apply for an International WILD Card which will give them 10 days' access to any of the 20 national parks within a single 15-day period. The cost (January 2004) is R600 for a single adult, R1 000 for a couple (any 2 adults) and R1 500 for a family (2 adults and up to 4 children).

Hout Bay: The spectacular view from Noordhoek Peak.

Back from the brink: Bontebok at Rhodes Estate.

Landmark: The Old Lighthouse at Cape Point.

GETTING WILD

■ Visitors should check SANParks' website – www.parks-sa.co.za – for details of the various WILD Card tariff options.
■ All current Go Green Cards are valid until expiry. The Go Green Card can be converted into a WILD Card.
■ For telephonic inquiries, use the Infinity Help Line number ℂ 086 123 4002, or SA National Parks Help Line numbers ℂ (012) 426-5011 or ℂ (012) 426-5013.
■ WILD Card applications can be processed directly by internet, www.endlessrewards.com/wild, or email wild@endlessrewards.com; fax (012) 654-4042.
■ Locally, WILD Card applications can be made at tourism offices at the Waterfront, ℂ (021)405-4500 or in the City, ℂ (021) 426-4260; at the Park's head office at Westlake, ℂ (021)701-8692; at Boulders, ℂ (021) 786 2329; at the Cape Point main gate ℂ (021) 780 9526; or at Buffelsfontein Visitor Centre, ℂ (021) 780 9204.

Ancient images: rock art on the walls of Peers Cave at Fish Hoek

THE PARK IN HISTORY

'THE FAIREST CAPE IN THE WHOLE CIRCUMFERENCE OF THE EARTH'

SIR FRANCIS DRAKE
ENGLISH NAVIGATOR, 1540-1596

The Park is most celebrated for its astounding floral diversity and glorious landscapes, but it also offers a rich cultural heritage stretching over millennia. The relics of the prehistory and precolonial eras are far less obvious and visible than those of the modern era, but are immensely significant in tracing the evolution of *Homo sapiens*.

Rock shelter: Booi se Skerm near Cape Point.

TRACES OF THE PENINSULA'S EARLY INHABITANTS

THE EARLY STONE AGE (ESA c.600 000 years ago) and Middle Stone Age (MSA c.200 000 - 30 000 years ago) inhabitants of the Peninsula have left a small number of artefacts from their fascinating history, like stone scrapers, hand axes and other fragments of stone tools which have been exposed in the odd wind-scoured depression near Cape Point and in middens – ancient refuse heaps – along the coast. However, much more is known about the lifestyles of these early people from archaeological excavations elsewhere, such as at Klasies near Humansdorp and Blombos Cave (MSA) on the southern Cape coast, although there are at least six MSA sites in the Cape Point section of the Park. There is more evidence of the simple lifestyles of the inhabitants of the Late Stone Age (LSA c.30 000 years ago) and of the later San hunter-gatherers and Khoekhoe pastoralists (▲ 11) who lived in the Cape Peninsula area from at least 2 000 years ago. This evidence, in the form of stone flakes and implements, shells and animal bones, skeletal remains and some pottery shards, has been found in more than 100 sites, including middens on the seashore and in rock shelters like Peers Cave (▲ 12) and in a cave at Smitswinkel Bay near the entrance to the Cape Point section of the Park. Limestone caves near Cape Point, like the Bynes and the evocatively named Booi se Skerm (Booi's shelter), are obvious shelters but have yet to be formally excavated.

All-in-all, very few physical remains of these early inhabitants can be seen *in situ* by latter-day visitors, other than some of the shelters themselves and shell middens scattered around the coast. But don't feel cheated – there is a considerable amount of material on display in museums around Cape Town that you can visit (▲ 14).

HISTORICALLY, THE SOUTH-WESTERN part of southern Africa was occupied for thousands of years by small groups of hunter-gatherers who were able to survive in all kinds of landscapes. Then, about 2 000 years ago, domesticated cattle and sheep reached the sub-continent, probably from tropical East Africa. The presence of this domestic stock gave rise to a distinct group in the south-western Cape: nomadic herders, some of whom referred to themselves collectively as Khoekhoen (or Khoikhoi) – this is a Nama word meaning "people". They were called Hottentots by the later European settlers. When Portuguese explorer Bartolomeu Dias reached Mossel Bay in 1488, he named it *Angra dos Vaqueiros*, Bay of the herders, because of the many domestic stock he saw there. The Khoekhoen in turn referred to the non-stock keeping hunter-gatherers by a variety of names, such as San, Sonqua or Obiqua – San is also a Nama word, while the other two were recorded by Van Riebeeck – while the Europeans referred to them as Bushmen. Today, the term Hottentot is considered derogatory, and while some have objected to the term Bushmen, it is now generally accepted. The inclusive term Khoisan is now commonly used to describe both the herders and the hunter-gatherers, indicating their common cultural and biological links and distinguishing them from the Nguni (Xhosa and Zulu) people. Some Khoisan prefer the spelling Khoe-San to clearly differentiate between the two groups.

There were many groups among the Khoisan, each with different names and languages or dialects – although all languages were

Artist's impression: A diorama at the Fish Hoek Valley Museum depicting early life in Peers Cave – the only site on the Cape Peninsula where rock art has been found.

characterised by clicks – but they shared important aspects such as rituals, religious beliefs and patterns of kinship.

It has been estimated that there were between 4 000 and 8 000 Khoisan living in the Cape area shortly before the arrival of the Europeans. At the beginning of the 17th century, European travellers reported that one group, numbering fewer than 100, lived on the shores of the Cape Peninsula and appeared to survive mainly on shellfish, certain roots and the flesh of beached marine mammals like whales. Dutch shipwreck survivor Leendert Janssen called them Strandlopers – literally, beach-walkers – and the name was commonly used at the time. The tribal name of the Strandlopers was *Goringhaicona,* and there is debate as to whether they were outcast Khoekhoen or former San hunter-gatherers subjugated by the biggest group of Khoekhoen at the Cape, the *Goringhaiqua*, who were called Kaapmans – literally, people of the Cape – by the settlers.

As the European settlement grew and the colonists expanded into the interior, they did so at the expense of the Khoisan, who were physically exterminated, forced into increasingly remote parts of the interior, or assimilated into the labour-based colonial economy. Introduced diseases, such as smallpox, also inflicted a major toll on the Khoisan. Both the *Goringhaicona* and the *Goringhaiqua* had virtually disappeared by 1720.

DIGGING DEEP INTO THE PAST

PEERS CAVE is a substantial, south-facing overhang in a rocky hill surrounded by sand dunes, in the middle of the Fish Hoek valley. It was first excavated by amateur archaeologists Victor Peers and his son Bertie, starting in 1927, although it had been previously rifled. The top layers provided evidence of the Khoisan hunter-gatherers who also used coastal resources like shellfish, and who fished, clubbed seals and ate the flesh of stranded whales. Artefacts included bone awls and arrow points, bored digging stick weight-stones, ostrich egg-shell beads, mother-of-pearl ornaments and fragments of woven reed. Further excavations about two metres down produced stone implements, including a few lance-heads and scalloped scrapers, dated between about 60 000 and 10 000 years old. The Peers family's most dramatic discovery was in 1929 when, at the deepest excavation, they found a skull with what appeared to be a notably different bone structure. Sensing its significance, Mrs Peers carried the skull home carefully in her own hat. Thought to be from the cave's oldest layers and described as the largest-brained human yet discovered, it was hailed as a major find of great scientific interest. Later, however, it became clear that while it was still very old (11 000 years), the burial shaft had been dug into the earlier deposits, and the skull, while robust, falls well within the modern range. Peers Cave was declared a National Monument in 1941. Unfortunately, it has been severely vandalised in recent years.

Exciting find: Victor Peers exhuming ancient human remains in Peers Cave.

The Peers Skull

Sifting the past: Victor Peers and his son Bertie excavate artefacts in the cave that was later named after them.

■ HUMAN SETTLEMENT IN THE PARK: PART II

The history of southern Africa took a dramatic turn in the latter half of the 15th century when the Portuguese explorers made their early voyages of discovery down the west coast of Africa, finally rounding Cape Point in late 1487 or early 1488.

Genteel outing: Victorian-era climbers pose on the Lion's Head chains.

THE START OF THE COLONIAL ERA

THE PORTUGUESE EXPLORERS (▲22) were followed by British and Dutch sailors, and the Cape quickly became a strategic stop-over because of its midway position on the long, arduous trade voyages to the East. Here the European fleets were reprovisioned with water, wood, and sheep and oxen bartered from the local Khoekhoe inhabitants. The Dutch East India Company (VOC) initiated the first European settlement at the Cape in April 1652, sending Jan van Riebeeck and 80 VOC employees to establish a permanent reprovisioning station. Over the next 200 years, the Dutch were joined by waves of French, British and German settlers, as well as other Europeans. Also, from 1658 until 1807 when the

'Portuguese explorers raising a cross': An archive drawing from an engraving of Bartolomeu Dias raising a cross near Cape Point in 1488.

trade was stopped, more than 60 000 slaves from West Africa, Angola, the East Indies and Madagascar were transported to the Cape (▲19). Slaves were finally emancipated in 1834. The relatively unexplored and under-emphasised story of slavery in South Africa is a key element in understanding the origins and persistence of Apartheid. Over time, the mix of cultures and races at the Cape engendered a unique society, a forerunner of the "Rainbow Nation" of South Africa today.

■ HUMAN SETTLEMENT IN THE PARK: PART III

Hout Bay's East Fort: The upper section, built by the British in 1796.

WHERE TO FIND OUT MORE

King's Blockhouse: On Devil's Peak..

For more information on the fascinating cultural history of the Park and of its surrounding areas, visit:

■ The Park's Buffelsfontein Visitor Centre near Cape Point. ✆ (021) 780-9204, on the Web: **www.cpnp.co.za** e-mail: **capepeninsula@ parks-sa.co.za**

■ The Iziko Museums of Cape Town, on the Web **www. museums.org.za/ iziko**
❏ SA Museum, Queen Victoria Street, in the city. ✆ (021) 481-3800;
❏ Slave Lodge, corner of Adderley and Wale Streets, city centre. ✆ (021) 460-8242;

■ Hout Bay Museum, Andrews Road. ✆ (021) 790-3270;

■ Bo-Kaap Museum, 71 Wale Street, in the city. ✆ (021) 481-3939

■ Fish Hoek Valley Museum, 59 Central Circle ✆ (021) 782-1752.

■ District Six Museum 25A Buitenkant Street ✆ (021) 461-8745

In contrast to the scarcity of *in situ* material relating to the lives of the original inhabitants of the Cape Peninsula, cultural artefacts dating from the time of the arrival of the first European settlers in the mid-17th century abound in the Park, and visitors with an interest in historical matters can choose from a wide array of highly intriguing sites.

Past glory: The ruins of the Queen's Blockhouse – one of three forts built on the slopes of Devil's Peak (▲ 110/1).

A RICH ARCHITECTURAL HISTORY

ONE OF THE PARK'S OLDEST historical sites lies deep in Newlands Forest: the ruins of an 18th century woodcutter's cottage, named Paradise. This cottage is most commonly associated with Lady Anne Barnard because she and her husband Andrew, secretary to the first British governor of the Cape, were offered it for use at weekends after arriving here in May 1797. Another is the King's Blockhouse, a stone fort of similar vintage (▲ 110/1). Constructed on the upper slopes of Devil's Peak by the British during the 1790s to ward off a possible attack on Cape Town from the south-east, it was later used as a prison for convicts helping with the afforestation of Table Mountain in the late 1800s. The blockhouse is still standing firm; however, it now contains communications equipment and is closed to visitors.

At the other end of the Peninsula, there is a historic farmhouse dating from the 1780s when the loan farm Buffelsfontein was granted to one Jeremias Auret – his land grant extended a half-hour's walk in all directions. The house, which became known as the Homestead during the later 20th century when it was a popular restaurant, has been faithfully restored and is now the Buffelsfontein Visitor Centre: the main information centre for the Cape of Good Hope section of the Park (▲ 136/7).

Historic image: An early artist's impression of Table Mountain seen from Table Bay.

Long exposure: A genteel visit to Woodstock Cave on Devil's Peak

Precarious: A ride on the cableway built for dam construction (▲ 21).

The Old Lighthouse at Cape Point, construction of which started in 1859 (▲ 132/3), and Maclear's Beacon, the highest point on Table Mountain dating from 1844 (▲ 19), are 19th century historic sites visited each year by hundreds of thousands of visitors. Ancient, very old, old or even relatively modern – when it comes to history, there's something for everyone in the Park.

Come to grief: The wreck of the Nolloth near Olifantsbos (▲ 26/7).

Great view site: The start of Chapman's Peak Drive on the Hout Bay side (▲ 30/31).

Ill-conceived: The Old Lighthouse at Cape Point (▲ 132/3).

Serene: Boulders Beach – long before the penguins arrived (▲ 138/9).

TABLE MOUNTAIN: PART I

Hoerikwaggo – "sea mountain" or "the mountain in the sea" – is what the indigenous Khoekhoe inhabitants of the Cape called Table Mountain and its companions: the present day Devil's Peak, Lion's Head and Signal Hill. Many of the Khoekhoen and their San (Bushman) counterparts must have climbed the mountain repeatedly over centuries, but the honour of the first recorded climb, in May 1503, has been assigned to a Portuguese navigator, Admiral Antonio de Saldanha.

ANCIENT CLAIM

The Greek historian Herodotus recorded that the Phoenicians had sailed around the Cape as long ago as 600 BC, but there is no evidence to support this claim.

A RARE GIFT INDEED

On World Environment Day 1998, then President Nelson Mandela declared Table Mountain a 'Gift to the Earth'.

A PLACE OF MANY NAMES

NEITHER OF DE SALDANHA'S famous predecessors from the previous century, explorers Bartolomeu Dias (1488) and Vasco da Gama (1497), stopped in the bay at the foot of *Hoerikwaggo* during their respective voyages of discovery, and several subsequent Portuguese fleets also passed it by. In 1503 De Saldanha anchored with his small fleet and climbed the mountain via Platteklip Gorge to check on what he believed was his pilot's faulty reckoning. Once he had proved him wrong – the incompetent navigator had incorrectly claimed they had already passed the Cape – he named the mountain he had just climbed *Taboa do Cabo*, or Table of the Cape: accurate and evocative. After De Saldanha's visit, the bay became known to the Portuguese as *Aguada de Saldanha*: the watering place of De Saldanha.

In 1601 the name Table was confirmed for the mountain and the same name was assigned to the bay, this time by the Dutch, who were having a few navigational problems of their own. A Dutch squadron commanded by Joris van Spilbergen sailed past a sheltered bay which they assumed was Aguada de Saldanha, but which was in fact the present Saldanha Bay, 80km to the north. They then dropped anchor in a bay that Van Spilbergen assumed was a new discovery, and which he recorded in his log as Tafel Baay (Dutch for Table Bay) on account of the

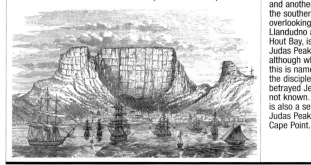

NO APOSTLES IN THIS RANGE

The line of buttresses running roughly south-west from Table Mountain above the Atlantic seaboard is called the Twelve Apostles, but in fact none of them is named after an Apostle, nor are there 12. The original Dutch name for this impressive set of buttresses was 'De Gevelbergen', meaning Gable Mountains, and acting British governor Sir Rufane Donkin is said to have bestowed the new name in 1820. Excluding buttresses on the Western Table of Table Mountain itself (Kloof, Cairn, Fountain, Fountain Peak and Grotto), the buttresses forming the Twelve Apostles are, from the north, Porcupine, Jubilee, Barrier, Valken, Kasteels, Postern, Wood, Spring, Slangolie, Corridor, Kleinkop, Grootkop, Separation, Grove and Llandudno Corner. One of the smaller peaks behind this line of buttresses is called St Paul and another, at the southern end overlooking Llandudno and Hout Bay, is Judas Peak, although whether this is named for the disciple who betrayed Jesus is not known. There is also a second Judas Peak, near Cape Point.

First encounter: Jan van Riebeeck meets the Khoekhoen on the lower slopes of Devil's Peak after his arrival at the Cape in April 1652.

"high hill, flat and square like a table" which dominated the bay.

Subsequently, the mountain became such an important navigational landmark on the long voyages to and from the East that the first sailor on a Dutch ship to sight its characteristic flat shape rising slowly over the horizon was awarded 10 gulden and a bottle of wine. In time, the Dutch named Devil's Peak "Windberg" – highly appropriate because of the raging south-easterly winds that whip over and around its summit – and they called Lion's Head "Leeuwen Kop" and Signal Hill "Leeuwen Staart" (Lion's Tail). These names were almost certainly on account of this outcrop's characteristic lion shape, rather than because of the actual presence of Cape lions.

Lure of the mountain: Excursions to Table Mountain have long been part of the way of life of Capetonians.

Abbé de la Caille

A STAR IN ITS OWN RIGHT

During his visit to the Cape of Good Hope (1750-1754), French astronomer Abbé Nicolas Louis de la Caille observed more than 10 000 previously unrecorded stars, and named many of the southern constellations. His particular tribute to Table Mountain was to name a constellation which he found near the Southern Cross in its honour: *Mons Mensa* (Latin for Table Mountain), with the nearby Large Magellanic Cloud representing the mountain's 'Table Cloth'. It is the only constellation named after a terrestrial geographical feature.

Mons Mensa: The constellation, marked out in red, is clearly recognisable as Table Mountain.

Landmark: An early photograph of Cape Town shows Table Mountain looming above the city.

LURED TO THE TOP OVER CENTURIES

THE ENGLISH HAD THEIR OWN IDEAS about names for *Hoerikwaggo* – "Mountain in the Sea". In 1620, commercial rivalry between themselves and Dutch traders using Table Bay for fresh supplies during their long voyages to the East caused two English seafarers, Andrew Shillinge and Humphrey FitzHerbert, to decide to annex Table Bay in the name of King James 1. They also re-named several of the local features: Signal Hill became "King James His Mount", Devil's Peak "Charles' Mount" in honour of Prince Charles (later King Charles 1) – an alternative version is that FitzHerbert immodestly named it "Herbert's Mount" – and Lion's Head became "Ye Sugar Loafe". But it seems that King James was not overly impressed with the new additions to his realm as the annexation was not confirmed, and neither did the new names stick.

For the next 20 years Table Bay was used exclusively by the English, and several sailors climbed "the hill called the Table". The first formal description of a climb was given by Peter Mundy, who summited in May 1634 with two companions via Platteklip Gorge which he described as "being like a valley but wondrous steep, the rocks on each side like monstrous walls, from which there is a continual distilling water".

The Dutch names for the various peaks were confirmed following the arrival of the first Dutch settlers under the command of Jan van Riebeeck in April 1652, although it was a full five months before any of his party managed to get to the top of Table Mountain.

From then on there was a steady succession of visitors to the summit, including naturalists, botanists, genuine travellers and a few eccentrics. Hardly any were prepared to spend a night out on the summit for fear of the ➤

A VERY PRECISE POINT ON TOP

In 1834, Irish astronomer Sir Thomas Maclear (1794-1879) was appointed Astronomer Royal at the Cape, and initiated the first geodetic survey of the region. In December 1844, as part of his survey for the verification and extension of the Arc of Meridian – calculated a century earlier by French astronomer Abbé Nicolas Louis de la Caille – he supervised construction of a three-metre rock beacon on the highest point of Table Mountain. This beacon, atop a rocky outcrop on the Eastern Table, was one of his three major survey points and was painted with lamp-black to make it stand out. Maclear's Beacon, as it came to be known, gradually fell into disrepair but was later restored, using the original stones, to commemorate the centenary of Maclear's death on 14 July 1979. It still marks the highest point on the Cape Peninsula. Initially recorded as 1 081m, the height was over subsequent years given variously as 1 085m, 1 086m and 1 087m, but has most recently – and most accurately – been measured at 1 088m. Devil's Peak is 1 002m high, and Lion's Head is 669m. Maclear's Beacon is now a National Monument. (▲108,112)

THE CIRCLE OF ISLAM

Not all visitors to the Peninsula and Table Mountain arrived willingly. Slaves were brought to perform forced labour from the outset of the new settler colony. Also, political 'trouble-makers' were exiled to the Cape from areas in the East controlled by the Dutch. Among the early exiles was a Goan prince of the Muslim faith, Sheik Yusuf, sent here in 1693. Sheik Yusuf's kramat (tomb of a Muslim holy man) at Macassar is one of six on the Peninsula and Robben Island, forming what Muslims refer to as the sacred Circle of Islam. They believe those living within the circle are protected from natural disasters such as fire, famine, plague and earthquakes. Another kramat, at Oudekraal, is that of Nureel Mobeen, a Muslim believed to have escaped imprisonment on Robben Island and who hid in caves of the mountain.

Sacred place: The kramat of Mohamed Gasan Galbie Shah on the saddle between Lion's Head and Signal Hill.

Majestic: An early view of Table Bay dominated by its mountains.

➤ lions, bears, tigers and other wild beasts of which many dwell in these valleys and crags", as one Nicolaus de Graaff wrote of his experience in March 1679. There were Lion at the Cape at the time, although probably not on the summit; the only potentially dangerous animals on the top were likely to be Leopard, and possibly also Spotted Hyena. Since these early days, literally millions of visitors have gone to the summit of Table Mountain – most of them, it must be said, by mechanical means in the cable cars. But, despite ecological, physical and social impacts on the most popular parts of the mountain which have changed some aspects considerably since those early hikers struggled to the summit, present day visitors still experience the same awe and excitement as they stand on the top and gaze out at the stunning views on offer all around them.

Astronomer: Sir Thomas Maclear

Ruins: Early hikers pose on the collapsed stones of Maclear's Beacon. It has since been restored. (▲108/9, 112)

19

AN INTIMATE ACQUAINTANCE

A VERY GENTEEL EXCURSION

One of the most prominent visitors to the summit of Table Mountain and the first woman to record her experience was Lady Anne Barnard. Her husband Andrew was Colonial Secretary during the first British occupation of the Cape (1795-1803). Lady Anne – dressed for the mountain outing in her husband's trousers and with her shoes tied on with metres of tape – undertook the three-hour ascent of Platteklip Gorge in July 1797. Also in her party were geologist and naturalist Sir John Barrow, two naval officers, her maid, and a dozen servants and slaves who carried their meal of meat, Port, Madeira and Cape wine, which they used to drink a toast to the King. 'We made a splendid and happy dinner after our fatigues,' she recorded. Unlike most other visitors of the time, they slept on the mountain and descended the next day.

'Earrings': Lady Anne was very taken with quartz pebbles on the top.

THERE ARE UNFORTUNATELY NO RECORDS of what the indigenous San and Khoekhoe inhabitants thought of their mountain, *Hoerikwaggo*. The first person who recorded all the moods of the mountain first-hand was Joshua Penny, an American sailor press-ganged into the Royal Navy in 1795.

As a crew member of HMS Stately, he took part in the Battle of Muizenberg that year. He then deserted, but was captured and put aboard HMS Sceptre in Table Bay. Desperate to escape, Penny feigned illness in October 1799, and once ashore gave his guards the slip and headed for the wilds of Table Mountain. He had just two loaves of bread, a calabash of brandy, a pair of duck trousers, a shirt, a Guernsey frock, a hospital cap, a flint and a knife. For the next 14 months, during which he had no human contact, he eked out a living in a cave high on Fountain Ravine, below the present Upper Cableway Station.

When he eventually ventured down, he discovered HMS Sceptre had sunk in a violent storm in Table Bay (▲ 26/7) just weeks after his escape – his decision probably saved his life. Back in America, he published a pamphlet in 1815, "The Life and Adventures of Joshua Penny", subtitled "Interspersed with many Curious Incidents and Hair Breadth Escapes". It was greeted with some scepticism, but in 1892 Mountain Club members rediscovered his cave and found several relics. In 1959 other club members found a flint box, four old buttons, the rusty remains of a knife and animal bones. All are now displayed in the Mountain Club of SA museum.

A STATESMAN WHO LOVED TABLE MOUNTAIN

The Smuts Memorial (▲ 112/3) was erected to honour General Jan Smuts, a keen conservationist and regular mountaineer who climbed the mountain aged 80 to give the keynote address at the Mountain Club's annual memorial service. The plaque contains the famous eulogy from Shakespeare's *Julius Caesar*:

'His life was gentle, and the Elements
So mixt in him, that Nature might stand up
And say to all the world, This was a man.'

AN ANCIENT SPELL

According to African legend Qamata created the world. However, Nganyamba – a mighty old dragon who sleeps under the sea – tried to prevent Qamata from creating dry land. To help him against Nganyamba, Djobela, the one-eyed earth goddess, cast a spell and created four giants, one each to guard the north, south, east and west. Many battles raged and eventually the giants were defeated. Before dying they asked Djobela to turn them into mountains so they could continue their work. The Watcher of the South – Umlindi Wemingizimu – became Table Mountain.
– as told by Credo Mutwa

Contained: Woodhead Reservoir, in front, and the Hely-Hutchinson Reservoir, behind.

TAPPING THE MOUNTAIN'S WATER RESOURCES

It was the presence of pure, life-giving water streaming off Table Mountain that first attracted human inhabitants to the area. The Khoekhoe name for what would eventually become Cape Town was *Camissa* – "Place of Sweet Waters". Despite various small canals and reservoirs built in the city area and fed from the stream in Platteklip Gorge, by the late 19th century Cape Town had expanded so quickly that a major dam on Table Mountain was necessary.

Workers during the dams' construction.

Pipers celebrate the opening of the dam.

In 1890, work started on the Woodhead Reservoir across the Disa River on the Back Table. In 1893, an aerial cableway was strung up Kasteel's Poort to get construction material to the top – the remains of the upper station of this cableway are still visible at Postern Buttress – and the cable car was an intimidating open skip. From this station, a railway line was laid to the dam site two kilometres away and a small steam engine, carried in pieces up the mountain, was used to haul material. The beautifully constructed stone wall of the dam is 248m long and 37.5m at it highest point, and its capacity is 995 megalitres. The last stone was laid by Mayor Sir John Woodhead in 1897, but within a year of its completion, Cape Town's water demand had outstripped supply and a second dam was constructed above it. The Hely-Hutchinson Reservoir, named after Governor Sir Walter Hely-Hutchinson, was opened in March 1904. Its stone wall is 532m with a maximum height of 15.1m, and it has a capacity of 924 megalitres. Wynberg, then an independent municipality, also constructed a series of reservoirs on the Back Table, further east. The Victoria Reservoir, completed in 1896, has a wall 6m high and a capacity of 128 megalitres; immediately below it is the Alexandra Reservoir, finished in 1903 with a 12.1m wall and a 126 megalitre capacity; and a third, the De Villiers Reservoir further down with a wall of 27.8m, overlooking Orange Kloof, was built in 1907. It has a capacity of 242 megalitres. An aerial cableway was built for the construction of these dams but it proved unsatisfactory and was replaced by a trolley track running up Rooikat Buttress from Kirstenbosch.

■ There is a comprehensive history of these dams in the Waterworks Museum, located in a building on the northern corner of the Hely-Hutchinson Reservoir. The museum is open on weekdays from 9am to 3pm and on weekends from 9am to 4pm. ✆ (021) 686-3408.

A SEA ROUTE TO THE EAST

ALTHOUGH THE CAPE PENINSULA had been occupied for millennia by indigenous inhabitants, it acquired new significance in the 15th century as European explorers, led by the Portuguese, tried to find a sea route to the East that would allow them to outflank the Islamic empire controlling trade in the Mediterranean basin. Foremost in this exploration was Portuguese nobleman Infante Dom Henrique (1394-1460), better known as Prince Henry the Navigator. After his death, his nephew, King John II, continued to promote voyages of discovery down the African coastline in the hope of finding India. One of his protegés was Bartolomeu Dias, who set sail from Lisbon in August 1487 with two caravels – small, lateen-rigged vessels – and a supply ship. Close to South Africa's present border with Namibia, Dias's tiny fleet was battered by strong winds and driven nearly 1 000km south. When they were finally able to turn east, they found only open ocean before them. And when they sailed north, eventually sighting land on 3 February 1488, they realised they'd "turned the corner" of Africa. Despite the undoubted excitement of this discovery which opened the way to the East, Dias's crew decided they'd had enough, and he was eventually forced to turn for home after erecting the first of three *padrãos* – limestone pillars bearing a cross and the Portuguese coat of arms, signifying Christianity and Portuguese sovereignty – at Kwaaihoek, some 100km east of the present Port Elizabeth.

On his voyage back, Dias stopped somewhere near Cape Point, and reportedly

Recent discovery: This cross, right, engraved in the soft calcareous rock near Cape Point, may mark the site where Dias erected a padrão while on the return leg of his famous voyage of discovery. It is still to be formally investigated.

A MATTER OF THREE CAPES

There are three capes at the southern tip of the Cape Peninsula, and the Portuguese probably used Cape of Good Hope as a generic name for this whole area. The most easterly of these capes is now called Cape Point, at 34 Deg 21' 24" South, 18 Deg 29' 51" East. The Cape of Good Hope, the most westerly of the three and some 2.2km from Cape Point as a seagull flies, qualifies by a fraction as the south-western-most point of the African continent, at 34 Deg 21' 25" South, 18 Deg 28' 26" East. In between the two is Cape Maclear, named after the one-time Astronomer Royal at the Cape, Thomas Maclear. Cape Agulhas is some 150km to the east (230km by road from Cape Town) and lies at 34 Deg 49' 58" South, 20 Deg 00' 12" East.

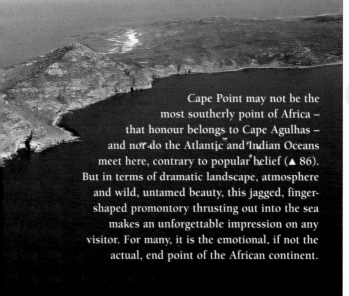

Cape Point may not be the most southerly point of Africa – that honour belongs to Cape Agulhas – and nor do the Atlantic and Indian Oceans meet here, contrary to popular belief (▲ 86). But in terms of dramatic landscape, atmosphere and wild, untamed beauty, this jagged, finger-shaped promontory thrusting out into the sea makes an unforgettable impression on any visitor. For many, it is the emotional, if not the actual, end point of the African continent.

Quincentenary: A modern replica of Dias's caravel rounds the Cape in 1988.

erected a second *padrão* on 6 June 1488. Unfortunately no first-hand account of his voyage exists – the earliest narrative of his journey is by 16th century chronicler João de Barros – and there is no certainty as to the exact location of this *padrão*. However, the recent discovery of a cross engraved on a rock in the Park which could point to its exact location, is now being investigated.

Dias reportedly named this area *Cabo Tormentosa*: the Cape of Storms, but when he reached Portugal and reported his discovery, King John was apparently so delighted at the prospect of its marking the way to the East that he re-named the southerly turning point *Cabo de Boa Esperança*, or the Cape of Good Hope. Continuing the proud tradition of exploration, Vasco da Gama set sail in July 1497 on the route discovered by Dias. He first sighted the Cape of Good Hope on 18 November. After rounding it four days later, he made his way up the east coast of Africa, where he found a pilot who took him to Calicut in India, arriving on 20 May 1498.

The long search for the lucrative sea route to the East was over, and the Cape of Good Hope had fulfilled the rich promise of its name.

AN INSPIRATION TO SAILORS THROUGH THE AGES

Stand on the rugged, 200m cliffs above Cape Point and take in the ever-changing seascapes below; sparkling Dias Beach and rough Cape Maclear off to the right; and the wide, gentle sweep of False Bay to the left – you will know exactly why the scribe of Sir Francis Drake, first sailor to circumnavigate the world, waxed so lyrical after they had rounded Cape Point on 18 June 1580: 'This cape is the most stately thing and the fairest cape we saw in the whole circumference of the earth.'

CAPE OF GOOD HOPE: PART II

EARLIEST DAYS AT THE SOUTHERN TIP

WHILE THE CAPE OF GOOD HOPE was an extremely important landmark and navigational aid to sailors, it remained largely isolated as far as human habitation was concerned. There is no record of when the last of the indigenous "Strandlopers" (▲ 11) left the area. Certainly they were still there in the early part of the 17th century, for French traveller Augustin de Beaulieu visited the Cape in 1620 and wrote a brief – and decidedly prejudiced – account of their lifestyle. But it is possible that by the early 18th century the southern tip of the Peninsula was effectively unoccupied.

The first farms in this area were granted in the late 1780s. But the soil here is not at all suitable for farming (▲ 45), and some of the landowners quickly turned to other activities, including fishing – at Buffels Bay, where there was trek fishing from the beach, and at Olifantsbos – and whaling: there was also an active whaling station at Buffels Bay. Another business was lime-making, stimulated by the building boom in Simon's Town. The main source of lime was an outcrop of calcareous stone between Buffels Bay and Booi se Skerm, where lime,

Disa racemosa: One of the loveliest of the many disas found on the Peninsula.

Simon's Bay was 'discovered' and named in 1687 by Simon van der Stel, one of the early Dutch governors. He appreciated its value as a sheltered anchorage, particularly from the fierce north-westerly storms in winter. Simon's Town developed from the 1740s, and it was not long after that the first loan farms were granted on the southern tip of the Peninsula, including Olifantsbos to Jan Hurter, and Buffelsfontein (site of the present Visitors' Centre) to Jeremias Auret.

Buffelsfontein: The original Smith's farmhouse. Now restored, it serves as the Park's main visitor information centre.

deposited as travertine, was quarried and burnt in kilns near Black Rocks and at Buffels Bay to produce good quality slaked lime for building mortar. The Black Rocks kiln, now restored, dates from about 1890. Another source of lime was mussel shells.

The Cape Point area became much more accessible after 1915, when the coastal road from Simon's Town to the Old Lighthouse at the Point was completed for security reasons relating to World War 1. But until the 1920s, the area was used mainly for recreation, and there were few buildings other than a handful of shacks. However, the threat of speculative development loomed, and had it not been for the foresight and generosity of two families and the tenacity of a great Cape Town naturalist, the Cape of Good Hope would have looked very different today. The Smith family had acquired Buffelsfontein farm in 1886, but by the late 1920s were considering selling. A land speculator was apparently interested, but the Smiths were not keen to sell to him. Dr SH "Stacey" Skaife, Cape Town's well-known naturalist, broadcaster and author, got

Chippy Baynes served as chief ranger of the newly established Cape of Good Hope Nature Reserve from 1942-59.

ENDANGERED

Witsenia maura, or Bokmakierie's Tail, resembles the tail of the bird of the same name. It is one of the Park's most endangered plant species.

24

to hear of this and started motivating for the farm to be bought as a nature reserve, because of its special ecology. Initially nothing came of Skaife's efforts, but in 1938, when the Smiths eventually had to sell, Skaife again led a campaign for official intervention. The Smiths turned down an offer of £20 000 by a Johannesburg consortium and agreed to sell for £16 000 if the farm was made into a nature reserve. Skaife mounted a public campaign with the help of the Cape Argus newspaper. Despite huge public support, the City of Cape Town refused to get involved, but fortunately the

Restored: The old lime kiln near Black Rocks.

Cape Divisional Council – the local authority responsible for the non-urban areas – was more enlightened, and on 11 April 1939 decided to purchase Buffelsfontein. An important addition was the Hare family's farm Blaauwberg Vlei, north-west of Buffelsfontein, which was already managed as a nature reserve and which was offered to the state on condition that it remained so – an offer gratefully accepted. The Cape Argus invited readers to submit names for the new reserve. After eliminating some fairly bizarre suggestions – like "Pixie Point" and "Bok-bok land" – the Divisional Council decided on 16 May 1939 it would be called "The Cape of Good Hope Nature Reserve".

Long gone: A view of Paulsberg and Judas Peak from the whaling station that operated in Buffels Bay.

Source of lime: The Bynes, a shallow cave system near Booi se Skerm, was eroded from soft calcareous rock.

SHOWING HIS IGNORANCE

No grass needed: The Cape Burrowing Scorpion

Arguing against buying the farm Buffelsfontein to create a nature reserve, Cape Town city councillor AZ Berman declared there was 'not enough grass to keep a scorpion alive'. Dr SH 'Stacey' Skaife (above), Cape Town's well-known naturalist who was motivating for the reserve, happily humiliated his opponent for his ignorance, pointing out that scorpions don't eat grass. In fact, they eat other invertebrates like beetles, grasshoppers, cockroaches and spiders.

25

◼ SHIPWRECKS

Look at a map of the Cape Peninsula and you will understand immediately why the 15th century Portuguese explorer Bartolomeu Dias named this coastline 'Cabo Tormentosa': the Stormy Cape, or Cape of Storms.

The frequent gale-force winds – particularly the north-westers in winter – and wild weather which batter the Peninsula have exacted a heavy toll over the centuries, and this coast is a veritable ships' graveyard. Crosses on the map mark wreck sites all the way down the exposed Atlantic seaboard and even in sheltered False Bay. Foundered ships like the *Het Huis te Crijenstein* (1698), *Visch* (1740), HNMS *Holland* (1786), *Le Napoleon* (1805), RMS *Athens* (1865), *Caterina Doge* (1875), *Nukteris* (1897), *Kakapo* (1900), SS *Umhlali* (1909), SS *Lusitania* (1911), *SA Seafarer* (1966), and *Katzu Maru* (2000) are just a few of a seemingly endless list.

Near disaster: Ikan Tanda, 2001

SHIPWRECK TRAIL

The trail starts at the Olifantsbos car park in the Cape of Good Hope section of the Park. It goes south along the coast, past the remains of the Thomas T Tucker and as far as Duikerklip and the wreck of the Nolloth. Hikers can either return from here or continue on a circular walk inland, where after about a kilometre the trail joins up with the Sirkelsvlei trail. (▲130) The walk takes about 90 minutes out and back, or between 2 to 3 hours for the circular route.

A TERRIBLE TOLL

ONE OF THE WORST STORMS to strike the Cape coast in modern times occurred on May 17 1865. Described variously, and with some understandable exaggeration, as "The Great Gale" and "the most disastrous gale that ever raged in the southern hemisphere", it drove ashore in Table Bay alone 17 sailing ships and the mail steamer RMS Athens with the loss of 60 lives. It was a similar wild winter's night in August 1909 when the liner Maori was forced onto the lee shore and struck a jagged rock off Duiker Point, below the Karbonkelberg near Sandy Bay with the loss of 48 lives. The wreck is now a favourite location for scuba divers.

The remains of five wrecks are still visible in the Cape of Good Hope section of the Park: Thomas T Tucker (1942), Nolloth (1965), Phyllisia (1968), Shir Yib (1970), and Tania (1972). The first two can be seen while walking the Shipwreck Trail (see box). The Thomas T Tucker was a 7 176-ton American Liberty ship on its maiden voyage from New Orleans to Suez with a cargo of war material for the Allied forces when it hit the shore at Olifantsbos in thick fog on the night of 28 November 1942. The captain reported that he had grounded on Robben Island, some 23 nautical miles (43km) to the north. The ship was a total wreck within hours, although all the crew were saved. An inquiry found the ship's compass was 37 degrees out.

The Nolloth was a 347-ton Dutch coaster which struck a submerged object – possibly Albatross Rock, 800m offshore – during the night of 10 April 1965. Its crew were rescued by a SA Navy helicopter. Dawn found the

Wrecked: From left, the Maori (1909) and the Romelia (1979), both near Llandudno; the crane Shir Yib near Cape Point (1970).

vessel hard aground at Duikerklip, just 500m south of the Thomas T Tucker. A customs team was sent quickly to the wreck site to retrieve the cargo which

Rusty remains: Debris from the Thomas T Tucker.

included a substantial amount of liquor, but rumour is that many bottles found their way into private hands. The Phyllisia was a 452-ton steam trawler which ran aground at Hoek van Bobbejaan on 2 May 1968, and the Tania was a small wooden trawler which went ashore just south of Buffels Bay in May 1972.

An unusual wreck was the 42m floating crane barge Shir Yib, which came ashore on rocks at Dias Beach below Cape Point in August 1970 after its tow from the British tug Britonia parted, again in heavy winter weather. Two seamen from the barge were rescued from the rocks, but two went missing, almost certainly drowned. The remains are still visible from the beach. Another floating crane which came to grief on the Park's coastline was the massive Dutch floating crane which also broke its tow and was driven ashore onto the rocks at Duikerpunt, between Sandy Bay and Hout Bay, in 1992. This wreck is still a prominent feature of the coast.

The Park had a narrow escape from a major pollution disaster in September 2001, when the bulk carrier Ikan Tanda ran aground just off the beach at Scarborough in extremely heavy seas (see picture, left). All of its crew were rescued. While Capetonians held their collective breath, salvors battled for a week to lighten the stricken ship, and there was a loud collective sigh of relief when it was finally pulled free and towed out to sea where it was sunk. Few things are certain, but it's a safe bet that the Cape of Storms has not yet claimed its last victim.

Hard aground: The Dutch floating crane ashore at Duikerpunt.

Wild place: The skeleton of the Nolloth on the Cape Point Shipwreck Trail.

Cape of Storms: The storm which wrecked HMS Sceptre. (▲20)

NEVER TO ROUND THE CAPE

The legend of the Flying Dutchman is one of the Cape's best-known tales. According to one source, the ship – a genuine Dutch vessel of this name commanded by a Captain Hendrik van der Decken – was struggling to make its way around the Cape in heavy weather in 1680 when it disappeared under the waves. But then legend took over, and the story now goes that the Captain had sworn a violent oath that he would get his ship around the Cape if he had to sail until Doomsday.

The Devil took the Captain up on his blasphemous assertion, and the old sailing ship is supposedly still occasionally seen during stormy weather, battling the elements but never succeeding in its quest to get past the Cape of Storms. One of the best publicised sightings of the Flying Dutchman was that by Britain's King George V in July 1881 when he was still the Prince of Wales and serving as a midshipman aboard HMS Bacchante. But, as author Mike Fraser points out, at that time the prince's Royal Navy squadron was just two days out of Melbourne, Australia – nowhere near the infamous Cape of Storms!

■ MINING THE MOUNTAINS

Loading zone: The jetty where manganese was loaded into ships in Hout Bay.

People arriving in new places have always entertained dreams of finding fabulous wealth in the form of precious metals and gemstones – gold, silver, diamonds or rubies, for example – and the European settlers who arrived at the Cape from the middle of the 17th century were no exception. The "El Dorados" did indeed materialise, but two centuries later and deep in the interior of the

country: around Kimberley (diamonds) and on the Reef in what is now Gauteng (gold). The Cape Peninsula is extremely poor in minerals; its fabulous treasure is in the more sustainable form of its unique floral wealth and unsurpassed scenic beauty.

Dreams of wealth: The Lion's Head 'gold' shaft.

THE FUTILE SEARCH FOR MINERAL WEALTH

THE FIRST DUTCH GOVERNOR Jan van Riebeeck had been at the Cape for less than two years when, in February 1654, he recovered what he thought was a small amount of silver from a piece of Table Mountain rock broken off for examination. The next day, he sent his silversmiths back onto the mountain to start digging at the site, but they found nothing, and, after further tests, pronounced the "silver" taken from his original sample to be not silver at all. The resulting disappointment was such that prospecting was put on the back-burner until the arrival of governor Simon van der Stel in 1679. After his return from a prospecting trip to far-off copper-rich Namaqualand in 1685, Van der Stel set his master miner Frederick Mattheus van Werlinghof to work looking for silver on the Peninsula. Van Werlinghof reportedly dug a 30m shaft on the slopes of the mountain at a now unknown location where he spent several months apparently only pretending to mine – obviously without success. He was replaced by another master miner, Gabriel Muller, who made a more serious effort, sinking a shaft in 1687 – still present but very overgrown, just above Ou Kaapse Weg – on the side of Steenberg mountain and also tunnelling in the valley below. He was equally unsuccessful. Although no silver was ever recovered from the "Zilwermijn" area, the name stuck, and it later became the Silvermine Nature Reserve. A small amount of manganese was mined in this area in later years.

Powder store: The Silvermine gunpowder magazine, which is still evident as a ruin.

GOLD HAS ALWAYS HAD MORE ALLURE than silver, and it was only a matter of time before someone either actually found this precious metal or pretended to do so. The first was a Captain Glendinning, who announced in February 1859 that gold had been found on his Camps Bay property. Then, in 1886, gold quartz was supposedly discovered on Lion's Head, creating a minor frenzy. Gold fever swept the city and prospectors swarmed over the mountainside. The Lion's Head Gold Syndicate prospected for some 18 months and sank a shaft reportedly about 45m deep, some 100m below the present start of the Lion's Head walk (▲ 102/3). The Lion's Head (Cape Town) Gold Mining Company was formed in December 1887 to carry on the work of the syndicate which it claimed had

There's a frequently repeated tale that the first load of ore from the Hout Bay manganese mine went careering out of control down the steep chute, off the end of the pier and straight through the hull of the waiting ship, sinking it. It is, however, a complete myth. From the end of the chute, the ore was transported along the jetty in cocopans, tipped into a barge, and then floated across to ships for export.

struck a gold reef about 5m wide. But despite frenzied efforts, no worthwhile deposits were found. Some quartz specimens were sent to Europe to be assayed, but the verdict was not encouraging and the mining stopped. In 1951, after a firefighter nearly fell into the shaft, the "gold mine" was filled in. A much more substantial mining operation was carried out by the Vredehoek Tin Company which produced cassiterite – oxide of tin – assayed at 70% – at "Prospect Hill" on the slopes of Devil's Peak in 1911/12.

Short-lived work: Miners at the manganese mine above Hout Bay.

At the height of this mine's activity, 100 men were employed and a shaft reportedly 60m deep was sunk. Later, a horizontal tunnel about 100m long was driven in to connect with the bottom of this shaft. It was a substantial operation, involving rock-crushing stamps, dams, and troughs for washing and separating the ore-bearing rock before export. But this mine also did not last long, and was abandoned after the machinery was removed. An equally substantial operation was the manganese mine in Hout Bay.

Starting in 1909, eight shafts were tunnelled on the mountainside above the East Fort, the longest of which reached some 84m into the mountain. The ore was transported down to the jetty in a 750m corrugated iron chute. But the operation was not sufficiently profitable, and this mine went out of business after two years. The only long-term mining on the Peninsula has been in the Noordhoek valley, where there are substantial deposits of high quality kaolin: a

Noordhoek's kaolin mine: The only mining still undertaken in the Peninsula.

white, clay-like material derived from the weathering of granite, which is used to manufacture china and in the production of other items, particularly paint and paper. In 2004 a big kaolin mine was still operating on the eastern slopes of Chapman's Peak. It is not within the Park borders.

■ CHAPMAN'S PEAK DRIVE

It was the cliff road that just about everyone in Cape Town thought could never be built. Certainly the Commissioner of Public Works was under that impression, because in March 1910 he wrote to the Cape Peninsula Publicity Association, telling them that a road between Hout Bay and Noordhoek along the sheer cliffs of Chapman's Peak was well-nigh impossible because of the ruggedness of this section of the mountain. It contained "features of extreme difficulty, there being in one section over a mile of perpendicular cliffs to contend with", he said. Noting that the cliffs dropped some 200 to 300 feet (about 70 to 100m) vertically into the sea, he added: "It would appear that no passage over this portion is practicable, even on foot."

Determined: Sir Frederick de Waal

NO SUCH THING AS 'IMPOSSIBLE'

BUT THERE WAS a small group of people who did not share his pessimism, and one of them was a man of considerable influence and determination who also just happened to enjoy road building: Sir Frederick de Waal, who was elected Administrator of the Cape shortly after the Commissioner's letter, in May 1910. De Waal – after whom De Waal Drive is named – thought a dramatic coastal road here would help attract visitors to the Cape when they tired of the then-popular tourist destinations like Egypt, and he employed mining surveyor Charl Marais to find a possible route. Marais, a perfectionist, thrived on the challenge of working in extreme conditions, which included being roped to the wall of the cliff at times and hiring a worker who cut footholds for him in the rock face and hacked out a platform for his theodolite.

Road builders: Convicts drafted in to build Chapman's Peak Drive took some seven years to complete it.

Scenic: Cars on the Drive before it was closed in January 2000. It was re-opened as a toll road in December 2003.

It was Marais who noticed the particular geological structure of Chapman's Peak that made the route a possibility. Here, the bottom formation of Table Mountain Sandstone – the Graafwater Formation, which consists of relatively soft intermingled layers of brown sandstone, pink siltstone and maroon-coloured shale – rests on a slightly rounded dome of Peninsula Granite (▲ 44/5). Marais correctly surmised that a road could be most easily carved out of the cliff face at this geological interface, with the required cuttings being made in the softer Graafwater Formation rocks.

Formidable: The sides of Chapman's Peak drop sharply into the sea.

BUT SUCH A PROJECT WOULD COST a lot of money, he warned De Waal – probably in the region of £20 000, an enormous sum in those days. But this was just the kind of challenge the Administrator thrived on, and he promptly both raised the required funds and also secured 700 convict labourers to do the hard and dangerous physical work.

Work began on the new road from the easier Hout Bay side in April 1915, and from the more difficult Noordhoek side 14 months later. Despite Marais's discovery, construction was still extremely difficult, and marred by repeated rockfalls and minor landslides. Chief engineer Robert Glenday has been hailed as the third main architect of this remarkable project, using relatively primitive tools and the largely unskilled – and doubtless unenthusiastic – workforce at his disposal to best advantage. The easier section between Hout Bay and Lookout Point took four years to finish, but it was another three years before the much more formidable section between Lookout Point and Noordhoek was complete. Finally, on 6 May 1922, Chapman's Peak Drive was officially opened by the Governor General of the then Union of South Africa, Prince Arthur of Connaught, who led a convoy of 160 motorcars and charabancs through a silk ribbon during a grand opening ceremony. The Drive became a major tourist attraction, but was volatile and dangerous, with rockfalls claiming several lives and causing serious injuries. Closed in January 2000, it was upgraded, with major new safety features, and re-opened as a toll road in December 2003.

LOCAL CONVICTS BUILT THIS ROAD

Good luck: Graffiti by the roadbuilders.

It's a popular Cape Town misconception that Italian prisoners of war helped build this road. In fact, they came nearly 30 years later, during World War 2, and worked on the pass through Du Toit's Kloof between Paarl and Worcester. As author Mike Lundy rightly points out, it would have been embarrassing to have employed Italian POWs on the Chapman's Peak project, because Italy fought on the side of the Allies during World War 1! The road was built with convict labour from the Cape.

Early visitors: The newly opened road.

■ THE RHODES ESTATE

Tribute: The memorial to Cecil John Rhodes.

Entrepreneurial genius, mining magnate, politician, the richest man in Africa, philanthropist, unashamed flag-bearer for the British Empire … Cecil John Rhodes (1853-1902) was a man of many parts. While history does not reflect kindly on all his achievements, Capetonians have reason to be extremely grateful to him. Without Rhodes, most of the natural area on the eastern slopes of Devil's Peak and Table Mountain – including Kirstenbosch – would almost certainly be under some form of development today, and the University of Cape Town would not enjoy its wonderfully privileged learning environment.

PUBLIC BENEFIT

Cecil J Rhodes

USING THE FORTUNE he acquired in the Kimberley diamond mines and scores of other business interests, Rhodes bought Groote Schuur on the slopes of Devil's Peak in 1891 and restored the building that was originally an old Dutch East India Company barn; it later became the official residence of South Africa's prime ministers. He also constructed several other mansions on the estate: Westbrooke and Welgelegen, as well as The Woolsack which was built for his close friend, the author and poet Rudyard Kipling. It was here that Kipling composed his well-known poem, *If*. In 1895, Rhodes bought the farm Kirstenbosch for £9 000. He also acquired Cecilia Estate, stretching from Kirstenbosch to Constantia Nek, and constructed what is now Rhodes Drive. After he died in 1902, these three properties – Cecilia, Kirstenbosch and Groote Schuur – were held in trust for the public in terms of his will, which was later legislated as an Act of Parliament. His estate, most of which was also left to the public, was worth some £6.5 million – an enormous fortune at that time.

THE RHODES MEMORIAL

The Rhodes Memorial was erected near the bench where Rhodes frequently sat in quiet contemplation, gazing at the view which he declared had no equal in the world. He wrote of Table Mountain: 'We people here broaden in our ideas and in our sympathies because we are always looking at the mountain.' The Memorial, modelled on a Grecian temple, was funded by public subscription and designed by Sir Herbert Baker, one of South Africa's most famous architects. It was officially opened in 1912 on

Rhodes's birthday, 5 July. At the foot of the Memorial is a large bronze statue of a horseman, *Physical Energy*, sculpted by George Watts, an admirer of Rhodes. Within the 'temple' is a bronze bust of Rhodes, sculpted by JM Swan. Under the bust a bronze plaque is inscribed with a tribute by Kipling:

The immense and brooding spirit still
Shall quicken and control.
Living he was the land, and dead
His soul shall be her soul.

Due for removal: Black Wildebeest did not occur here historically.

A PARKLAND OF PROBLEMS

FROM THE TIME that Rhodes acquired and consolidated the Groote Schuur Estate, large sections of it have been managed as an artificial parkland. Alien trees like Cluster Pines (*Pinus pinaster*), other pines and various oak species were planted, and paddock areas, or camps, were established for grazing animals through the introduction of non-indigenous grasses. Indigenous, but not all locally occurring, animals (▲ 66/7) like Eland, Black Wildebeest and Mountain Zebra were brought in to create a "safari-like" atmosphere, and exotic species like the Fallow Deer and Sambar were also introduced. However, grazing in the camps was too poor to support the large antelope throughout the year and they suffered from a lack of protein and trace element deficiency, sometimes resulting in mortality. As a result, the Eland were all

Gone: Eland have been removed as the grazing is too poor for their needs.

removed, and there are plans to relocate the Black Wildebeest, which did not occur here historically, as well as the alien deer. This lower part of the former estate has been permanently transformed from its original renosterveld vegetation, and it will be managed as a cultural historical landscape, with the reintroduction of indigenous small animals and the upgrading of paths and tracks so visitors can access it more easily.

THE QUAGGA PROJECT

Not quite like mom: A foal born at Groote Schuur Estate shows reduced striping.

The Quagga was generally thought to be a distinct zebra species, *Equus quagga*, characterised by a basic brownish colour and much reduced striping. Mercilessly hunted by the European settlers, it was driven to local extinction in the mid-19th century and the last of its kind, a mare, died in Amsterdam Zoo in August 1883. That might have been the end of the Quagga story, but for Reinhold Rau of the South African Museum in Cape Town. Based on his research into the remaining 23 preserved Quagga skins in institutions around the world and aided by major advances in genetic science, DNA from tissue collected during the remounting of several stuffed museum specimens was analysed in the early 1980s. This proved conclusively that the Quagga had the same genetic make-up as its more northern cousin, the Plains Zebra which still exists today. So by using standard animal husbandry breeding techniques, the Quagga – now known as *Equus quagga quagga* – can be re-bred from the Plains Zebra, *E. quagga burchelli*. The Quagga Project was initiated in 1987, aimed at reversing this animal's extinction. The Groote Schuur Estate section of the Park is one of the selected breeding areas which have already produced very exciting results. SA National Parks is a major partner in this project, and other 'quaggas-in-the-making' are being bred in the Karoo National Park (▲ 164/5), and at Vrojlikheid nature reserve near Robertson and on private land. For more details: **www.museums.org.za/sam/quagga/quagga.htm**

Extinct: The last known Quagga died in a zoo in Amsterdam in 1883.

33

■ CREATION OF THE PARK

Invader: Spanish Broom

Although the first human inhabitants of the Peninsula had an impact on their splendid surroundings – particularly through their use of fire – the ecological effect of this was minimal compared to the devastation that followed the arrival of the European settlers in the 17th century. Wood-cutting, flower picking, ever-encroaching human development, the damming of rivers, mining, farming, quarrying, afforestation, the introduction of invasive alien species and numerous uncontrolled fires – all caused untold environmental damage like erosion and loss of biodiversity to the Cape Peninsula and its famous mountain chain.

Devastating: Wildfires started by people are a constant threat.

Special challenge: The Park is surrounded by dense human settlement.

Urban encroachment: Housing in the floodplain of the Silvermine River at Fish Hoek has forced engineering of the estuary.

A LONG TIME IN THE MAKING

THE FIRST FORMAL CONSERVATION of any part of the Peninsula was only in 1939 when the Cape of Good Hope Nature Reserve was proclaimed at the southern tip (▲ 22/5). Twelve years later, in 1951, the Van Zyl Commission was appointed to investigate the preservation of Table Mountain as a national asset. Unfortunately it rejected the idea of a single controlling authority, although its recommendations led to the establishment of a co-ordinating advisory authority, the Table Mountain Preservation Board. But this board lacked teeth and degradation continued.

The conservation goal was advanced significantly when the City of Cape Town proclaimed the Table Mountain Nature Reserve in 1963 and the Silvermine Nature Reserve in 1965, conserving much of the mountain north of Fish Hoek. But despite excellent conservation work here and at the Cape of Good Hope Nature Reserve, overall the mountain continued to deteriorate. The real wake-up call came in a hard-hitting report in 1976 by University of Cape Town botanists Eugene Moll

Australian Acacias: Invading plants like these are one of the biggest threats to the Park.

and Bruce Campbell, "The Ecological Status of Table Mountain". They said the situation whereby publicly-owned natural areas of the mountain were managed by 14 different bodies was totally unsatisfactory, and that the whole area should be controlled by a single authority. Their appeal generated considerable debate, and in 1977 Dr Douglas Hey, director of Cape Nature Conservation, was appointed as a one-person commission of inquiry into the

Wall-to-wall: Alien plants introduced by the colonists devastated natural ecosystems.

"Future Control and Management of Table Mountain and the Southern Peninsula Mountain Chain". He concluded the then National Parks Board was capable of managing the mountain but most landowners would not voluntarily co-operate and expropriation would be costly and deeply divisive. Instead, he proposed a federal management system with all authorities voluntarily subscribing to a uniform management policy. This led to the formation of the Cape Peninsula Protected Natural Environment (CPPNE) management advisory committee.

It was only during the 1990s that the possibility of a national park – the country's highest conservation status – on the Cape Peninsula attracted serious political support. However, many Capetonians remained deeply suspicious of "outsiders from Pretoria", as the National Parks Board was viewed. Fortunately the advent of democracy in 1994 led to fundamental changes in both national and local government. This, combined with growing environmental awareness, intense lobbying by conservation groups, and the replacement of the parks board with the more representative SA National Parks, was sufficient to turn

Blighted landscape: The quarry at Glencairn.

the tide of opinion. In December 1995, both the national and the Western Cape cabinets approved in principle the establishment of the Cape Peninsula National Park, but it still took hard bargaining to make it a reality in 1998. In 2004 it was renamed Table Mountain National Park (Intaba Yetafile iPaka Kazwelonke in Xhosa and Tafelberg Nasionale Park in Afrikaans).

ℹ MILESTONES OF THE PARK

■ 1958: All land on Table Mountain above the 500-foot (152m) contour line is declared a National Monument.

■ April 1998: An official Cape Peninsula National Park signing ceremony is held at Kirstenbosch.

■ 29 May 1998: the first 14 000ha of the Park is proclaimed in the Government Gazette.

■ 2004: The Park is renamed Table Mountain National Park.

Table Mountain National Park is unique, because it both conserves elements of the globally important Cape Floral Kingdom and is one of only a handful of national parks anywhere in the world located entirely within a major metropolitan area. Because South Africa is a developing nation with a long history of inequality, the Park's duty is to conserve the Peninsula's rich biodiversity while at the same time making a meaningful contribution to the socio-economic development of citizens living on and around its borders.

■ CAPE TOWN STATISTICS

- Area of Metropolitan Cape Town: 2 487 km²
- Estimated population: about 3.3 million (2003)
- Population growth rate 2001-2006 – approx. 2.1% per year
- Unemployment: at least 20% of the economically active population
- Formal employment (2001 Census) 867 052
- Informal employment (2001) between 145 000 and 240 000

MEETING MAJOR CHALLENGES

CAPE TOWN ENJOYS the highest economic growth rate in South Africa – about 3% – and employment levels exceed the national average. Tourism generates more than R11 billion annually for the city, or about 10% of gross geographic product (GGP), and employs more than 50 000 people. The city's tourism employment ratio is 1:19 – above the national average of 1:29 but well below the international average of 1:8.

Like all South African cities and many other cities elsewhere in the world, Cape Town also has major development challenges, and still has unacceptably high

Popular: The Boulders penguin colony.

Work for all: Clearing invasive alien vegetation and other ecological restoration work has created hundreds of jobs for disadvantaged communities living on the Park's borders.

levels of unemployment of at least 20%. And because of perceived economic opportunities, it continues to attract major migration from the rural areas. If the unemployment rate is to be reduced and an acceptable quality of life is to be achieved for all its 3.3 million inhabitants (2003 estimate), it needs to attain an estimated annual growth of 7% in its GGP.

The Park is able to play a major role in efforts to attain this required growth, because many of Cape Town's top tourist destinations are within its borders. Hence it is a significant generator of income and a provider of employment opportunities for the city – and particularly for the historically disadvantaged citizens. So it is not surprising that the City of Cape Town – the Park's primary partner – and other funders have made huge investments in the financial sustainability of the Park.

The total cost of running the Park from 1998 to 2003 was R225 million, of which the city contributed R56 million with another R66 million coming from GEF (Global Environment Facility) and FFEM (French Global Environment Facility). The funders' investment gave the Park the opportunity to engage in economic empowerment opportunities through the appointment of previously disadvantaged contractors to do invasive alien plant clearing and footpath maintenance. From 1998 to 2003, the Park employed about 300 people on these programmes.

CAPE TOWN'S TOP TOURIST ATTRACTIONS

(Not in order)
- Table Mountain
- Cape Point
- Waterfront
- Boulders penguin colony
- Kirstenbosch botanic gardens
- Cape winelands
- Robben Island
- Chapman's Peak Drive
- Beaches
- Township tours

SOUTH AFRICA'S TOP TOURIST ATTRACTIONS

- Cape Town Waterfront
- Table Mountain
- Cape Point
- Cape winelands
- Kirstenbosch
- Garden Route
- Ostrich farms
- Kruger National Park
- Durban beachfront
- Robben Island

■ Fog rolls in around Lion's Head. (▲102)

■ A Southern Right Whale off the Peninsula. (▲90)

■ An Orange-breasted Sunbird finds nectar in an Erica. (▲78)

■ A porcupine at Cape Point. (▲66)

■ Late afternoon light on Noordhoek Beach. (▲128)

■ The Sentinel and Karbonkelberg behind Hout Bay. (▲30)

■ The Table Mountain Ghost Frog (▲ 72/3)

■ Soft coral (▲ 86/7)

■ Wild Almond fruit (▲ 115)

40

ECOLOGY OF THE PARK

'MAY YOU BE
FULLY AWARE
OF YOUR
FORTUNATE LOT
TO ENJOY THAT
PARADISE ON
EARTH, THE CAPE
OF GOOD HOPE'

LINNAEUS
SWEDISH BOTANIST & TAXONOMIST,
1707 – 1778

■ April Fool or Blood Flower
(*Haemanthus*) (▲126)

FOUR SEASONS IN ONE DAY

A SMOKY TALE

Although the exact origin of the name Devil's Peak is now lost, it is bound up in the popular legend of Van Hunks, a local variation of an old Dutch moral tale about smoking, cleverly incorporating a local weather phenomenon: frequent thick cloud billowing around the Saddle area between Devil's Peak and Table Mountain. Van Hunks was a retired pirate who enjoyed sitting on the Saddle and puffing up a cloud of smoke from his long-stemmed clay pipe. One day a stranger joined him and asked for tobacco. Van Hunks obliged, the talk about smoking grew boastful, and the man challenged Van Hunks to a duel. After several days of furious puffing, in which a huge cloud enveloped Devil's Peak, the angry stranger conceded defeat, but then revealed himself as Satan and whisked Van Hunks to Hell. There are several variations of this tale, including that the Devil arrived to claim the old sinner, but that Van Hunks tried to delay the inevitable by suggesting a smoking contest with his soul as the stake; the game – and hence the 'smoke' – has continued ever since. To this day, whenever there's cloud over the Saddle, locals say Van Hunks is still enjoying his pipe.

CAPE TOWN IS FAMOUS – some might say infamous – for two of its weather systems: the "Cape Doctor", or summer's south-easterly winds which often reach gale force; and the cold fronts which sweep across the Peninsula in regular procession in winter, driven by fierce north-westerly gales and bringing driving rain. These two systems have a profound effect on the Cape Peninsula and have shaped its ecology; at Cape Point, for example, which is the most exposed place on the South African coastline, the flora has to cope with an annual average – average, note! – wind speed of 8.5 metres per second, or just over 30 km/h. However, it's incorrect to suggest that these two wind patterns totally dominate the local weather. There are many days in all seasons – particularly spring and autumn, but even in mid-winter between fronts – when the sun shines out of a clear blue sky; when the temperature is warm and balmy; and when the wind, if there is any, is but a gentle breeze. These are the days that are just made for exploring the Park. Technically, the Cape Peninsula has what meteorologists term a Mediterranean climate: a long, warm, dry summer and a short, cool, wet winter, when most of the annual rain falls. Because of its proximity to the sea and low average altitude, the Peninsula never gets really hot or very cold; the record high is 41°C, and the lowest the mercury has fallen is -1°C – barely cool by the harsh standards of many other places in the world. The annual average daily temperature is a mild 22°C. But this can be deceiving, because ➤

Unusual display: Swirling clouds catch the evening light over Cape Town

THE CAPE DOCTOR
The infamous south-easter can blast down the mountainside at speeds of 130 km/h. While annoying to many Capetonians, it clears the city of heat, smog and flying insects – hence its colloquial name, the Cape Doctor. One ancient tale about the south-easter tells of how a young San (Bushman) hunter, alerted to a fire on its slopes, called to Kaggen, the Mantis God, to help. Kaggen pulled out a huge white karos – an animal pelt, and image for the cloud – from his mountain cave and used it to quell the blaze.

Rain coming: According to Cape Town's weather folklore, rain is imminent if Lion's Head is shrouded in low cloud. This is not an infallible prediction, but it is based on long observation and is an indication of likely showers.

➤ the Peninsula's particular physical shape creates micro-climates and mini weather patterns that differ substantially over short distances. For example, Newlands receives nearly four times as much rain annually as Cape Point. In high summer, visitors to the Oudekraal picnic site could enjoy a scorching, wind-free day while those on the nearby summit of Table Mountain could be blanketed in a wet, icy shroud of thick south-east cloud.

Visitors to the Park must always be prepared for the proverbial "four seasons in one day", particularly if they are moving between different areas. It is advisable to carry a hat or cap and warm, windproof clothing at all times, even in mid-summer.

	TEMPERATURES (CENTIGRADE)			RAINFALL
	Highest Recorded	Av. Max	Av. Min	Av. Month
Jan	39°	26°	16°	15mm
Feb	38°	27°	16°	17mm
Mar	41°	25°	14°	20mm
Apr	39°	23°	12°	41mm
May	34°	20°	9°	69mm
Jun	30°	18°	8°	93mm
Jul	29°	18°	7°	82mm
Aug	32°	18°	8°	77mm
Sep	33°	19°	9°	40mm
Oct	37°	21°	11°	30mm
Nov	40°	24°	13°	14mm
Dec	35°	25°	15°	17mm

TABLE MOUNTAIN'S FAMOUS "TABLE CLOTH" forms when moisture-laden air is blown in from the sea by the strong south-easterly winds and condenses in the cooler temperature as it is forced higher by the mountain. Then, when it tumbles over the edge, it dissipates again as it meets the warm air rising from the City Bowl. Precipitation from the cloud clings to plants, leaving behind more than twice as much water as actually falls as rain on the summit and surrounding areas. This water then filters down into cracks and fissures in the mountain sandstone, replenishing the water table. Dr Rudolf Marloth (▲49) undertook the first experiment to measure the amount of precipitation deposited by cloud on Table Mountain.

■ GEOLOGY

THE START OF IT ALL

Fantastical: Smith's Rock at Cape Point.

THE CAPE PENINSULA is composed of three major rock formations of different ages.

The oldest is the Malmesbury Group, consisting of dark grey mudstones and lighter coloured sandstones deposited as sediments into a marine environment which geologists call the Adamastor Ocean after the mythical Greek giant. This was the predecessor of the current Atlantic Ocean. The Malmesbury Group, deposited over a lengthy period ending some 540 million years ago, is often deeply weathered. It underpins most of the City Bowl and is clearly seen along the Sea Point shoreline, on Signal Hill and on the lower slopes of Devil's Peak, where it has weathered into a relatively rich clay soil.

The second oldest formation is the much harder, coarse-grained Cape granite, with large white feldspar crystals, glistening flakes of black mica, and grey glassy quartz. This rock has its origins in the closing of the Adamastor Ocean about 540 million year ago, when a convergent, or collisional, plate boundary was formed between two tectonic plates. One plate was subducted – forced under the other – and at depths of several hundred kilometres became so hot that it melted, rose, cooled and crystallised as granite deep within the continental crust when bodies of granitic magma (molten rock) rose towards the cooler surface. In the Cape Peninsula, this granite intruded into the cooler country rock – the Malmesbury Group (see "Darwin" box, at right). Granite forms a solid foundation for most of the Table Mountain chain, and huge granite outcrops can be seen on Lion's Head, along the Atlantic seaboard, below

Exposed: The Graafwater Formation sandstones on Chapman's Peak Drive.

❗ OLDER THAN THE SWISS ALPS

Table Mountain is one of the oldest mountains in the world. The Alps were only created some 32 million years ago; the Himalayas 40 million years ago; and the Rockies 60 million years ago. The modern Andes in South America were formed during two major uplifting episodes, 45 and 15 million years ago respectively.

Chapman's Peak Drive, and on the eastern Peninsula at Boulders, among other places in the Park.

The third major rock group is the Table Mountain Group. Over a period of about 20 million years, both the Malmesbury Group and the Cape Granite were planed off, probably by rivers. Then, from about 520 million years ago, the first sediments of the Table Mountain Group were deposited. Geologists interpret the Table Mountain Group in the Cape Peninsula as comprising three formations: a set of fine sandstone and mudstone beds of the 25m to 65m thick Graafwater Formation, coloured red and purple; pebbly, light grey, coarse sandstones of the younger, 700m thick Peninsula Formation, forming the bulk of the mountain as we know it today; and

PENINSULA FORMATION

GRAAFWATER FORMATION

CAPE GRANITE

THE PLACE WHERE DARWIN MARVELLED

About 540 million years ago, molten granite fused in some places with the heat-softened, older Malmesbury Group, creating an extraordinary belt of mixed rock or migmatite, known as the Contact Zone. This can be seen at the bottom of Beach Road in Sea Point – a famous geological site first noted in 1808 and visited since by many scientists, including Charles Darwin in 1836 when he was a scientist aboard HMS Beagle's famous voyage of scientific inquiry.

Geological wonder: Pale granite intrudes into the darker mudstone in this ancient contact zone at Sea Point. The mudstones have been baked into spotted hornfels.

POOR SOILS FOR FYNBOS PLANTS

Table Mountain Group Sandstone is hard and it erodes slowly, producing sandy, nutrient-poor soils that are easily leached. These soils are at the heart of the mountain's ecology; hence most fynbos plants contain few nutrients and make for poor grazing, which is why there are few big herbivores in fynbos. Soils derived from Cape granite and the Malmesbury Group rocks weather more easily and are also much richer in nutrients.

thirdly, on the very top of Table Mountain, the glacially derived Pakhuis Formation (see box, right). About 250 million years ago, the Table Mountain Group was folded and faulted during the "Cape mountain building episode". When the super continent Gondwana broke up about 130 million years ago, the Peninsula was block-faulted into several giant blocks. One fault, for example, runs through the Fish Hoek valley, and another from Smitswinkel Bay through to Scarborough. About 60 million years ago, Table Mountain had probably assumed something like its present shape. Gradually the overlying strata eroded off the top of the mountain – it might have been twice as high, but geologists have no way of knowing with any certainty – and the Peninsula and Pakhuis Formations were exposed. Continuous erosion will eventually flatten the mountain, but not for another 10 million years or so.

WHY IS TABLE MOUNTAIN FLAT?

It's not really flat, only flattish on the front section. Its predominant rock type – Table Mountain Group Sandstone of the Peninsula Formation – is a sedimentary formation that was laid down in successive layers over aeons. When Gondwana split up about 130 million years ago, the Peninsula was block-faulted into several massive blocks. None of these blocks is perfectly horizontal, but Table Mountain itself is hardly tilted and is almost horizontal, with individual sandstone beds causing the 'flat' top of the mountain. About 440 million years ago, glaciers brought down glacial gravel and sand of the Pakhuis Formation. Remnants of this glacially deposited formation are preserved near Maclear's Beacon on the summit of the mountain. Here, pebbly sandstone can be found, with pebbles containing glacial scratch marks.

On the Web: **www.uct.ac.za/depts/geolsci**; **www.geoscience.org.za/bellville/**

45

■ CAPE FLORAL KINGDOM: PART I

Fynbos specialists: The distinctive Green Protea Beetle (*Trichostetha fascicularis*), right, and the delicate Fynbos Blue Butterfly (*Tarucus thespis*).

Welcome to the world's richest natural garden!

That claim may come as a surprise to many visitors and local residents alike, who are sometimes disappointed at the apparently dry, drab and uninteresting vegetation they see as they drive, cycle or even walk through the Park, particularly during mid- to late summer. But the truth is that they are in the heart of one of Nature's jewels: the Cape Floral Kingdom, one of only six floral kingdoms in the entire world, and also the smallest and – proportionate to size – by far the richest. It is easily persuaded, through a little careful looking, to reveal its myriad charms and secrets.

A FINE AFFAIR

Fynbos (pronounced 'fain-bos') is an Afrikaans word derived from the Dutch phrase *fijn bosch*, meaning literally fine bush, and there are two possible explanations for its origin. Many, but certainly not all, of the plants which characterise this region have fine, narrow leaves, the shape of which helps reduce evaporation and prevents desiccation during the long, hot summers. Hence fynbos could be referring to the physical appearance of the 'typical' plants of the region. Another interpretation is that while the first Dutch settlers at the Cape in the mid-17th century found some exploitable wood in the Peninsula at places like Newlands and Hout Bay, most of the local vegetation had timber which was too slight or fine to be harvested, hence it became known as *fijn bosch*. Whichever is correct, fynbos has become the popular generic name for the vegetation type of the Cape region, although some plant families which also occur here are, botanically speaking, not fynbos.

Restio: There are about 330 restio species in fynbos.

King Protea

Every colour of the rainbow: Pincushions, pink everlastings, *Heliophila*.

At the heart: Restios are the defining plant of fynbos.

UNIQUE SPLENDOUR

Disa maculata

Mimetes fimbriifolius

FLORAL KINGDOMS are derived from the number of plant species, genera and families which are endemic – that is, that grow naturally only there and nowhere else in the world. For example, one of the six plant kingdoms is the Boreal Kingdom which covers the whole of the northern hemisphere. The Cape Floral Kingdom – usually simply called fynbos – is a tiny, crescent-shaped floristic region covering less than 90 000 sq km, stretching from about Vanrhynsdorp in the north, taking in the Cape Peninsula and the southern Cape plains in the south, and extending east as far as Grahamstown in the Eastern Cape. In places this extraordinary crescent of life is just 40km wide, and nowhere is it more than 200km from the sea. Crammed into this area – which comprises just 0.04% of the world's land surface! – are an

astonishing 8 578-plus plant species, of which just under 70% are endemic, as are 193 (20%) of its 955 plant genera, as well as six plant families. Nowhere else in the world is there such profusion of endemism and concentration of species: per 10 000 square kilometres, fynbos has on average 1 300 different plants – more than three times the equivalent (400 species) of the Brazilian rainforest. In one fynbos patch measuring just 10 metres square, botanists recorded 121 plant species. Many fynbos plants have minute natural ranges: one erica, for example, grows only in a single hectare of the Park. One orchid is known only from two cliff ledges, also in the Park; another occurs in an area of less than one hectare near Cape Point. Although still present in 2004, this orchid had last flowered 26 years ago.

Pypie: *Gladiolus brevifolius,* one of 17 gladiolus species in the Peninsula.

Pelargonium

I **Familiar favourite:** Many popular horticultural plants like pelargoniums – the wild parents of geraniums which grace so many window boxes around the world – gladiolus, freesia, daisy, lily, iris and several other bulbous species have their origins in fynbos.

atsonia

Fire Heath

Silver Tree

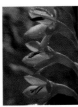

Watsonia

Gladiolus

1.*Lachenalia aloides*; 2.Conebush (*Leucadendron* sp);
3.Everlasting; 4.March Lily; 5.Leucadendron; 6.Blue Disa

Gladiolus

Much of the northern hemisphere was subjected to a severe ice age relatively recently – it only ended about 100 000 years ago – which effectively wiped out its entire plant life. Southern Africa, in contrast, has not been disturbed by such violent glacial forces in recent geological time. Fynbos, therefore, is an ancient vegetation type, with many of its plant families developing over the past two to three million years, or even longer in the case of restios (reeds) which are among the oldest plants of the region – some date back more than 60 million years! This ancient lineage of fynbos, combined with the large number of different landscapes and micro-habitats within the fynbos region, help account for its incredible diversity and number of plant species.

Leucadendron sp
(Knoppiesbos)

THE HOTTEST OF HOTSPOTS

Fynbos, or the Cape Floral Kingdom (some scientists prefer to talk about the Cape Floristic Region) has been described as 'among the very hottest of the world's biodiversity hotspots'. This means that while it is among the richest of the world's depositories of life forms – particularly plants and insects – it is also among the most threatened, for many reasons such as human development, frequent fires and the spread of invasive alien species. More than 1 400 fynbos plants feature in the Red Data Book as being critically rare, endangered, threatened or vulnerable. At least 29 of these plants are known to be extinct, including several on the Cape Peninsula. Following the proclamation of the Park in 1998, there is now a much better chance of dealing with these threats and ensuring the survival of the wonderful biodiversity that remains in the natural areas of the Peninsula section of the Cape Floral Kingdom.

A UNIQUE COMBINATION

Syncarpha vestita: Everlastings abound in summer.

FYNBOS HAS FOUR MAIN GROUPS of plants or growth forms: proteas, characterised by tall shrubs with broad leaves; ericas, the smaller heath-like shrubs; restios, or reed-like plants; and geophytes, or bulbous soft-stemmed plants.

In some fynbos types, either proteas or ericas – or sometimes both – can be scarce or even absent. The 1 400-odd bulb species – the richest geophyte flora in the world – appear during the wetter months, and particularly in spring and after fire; during the dry summer months they are virtually invisible in the landscape. It is only the restios which occur in all the different fynbos habitats; restios, therefore, are the defining, or uniquely

3 4 5 6

Fynbos glory:
A stand containing three of the four fynbos elements: restios, ericas and leucadendrons (Protea family).

distinguishing, plants of fynbos. The vast majority of Africa's 330 restio species occur in the Cape.

All plant communities are influenced by, and owe their very existence to, a unique combination of physical and biological factors. Some communities, like the savanna, are particularly influenced by biological factors – for example, the presence of huge numbers of grazing animals feeding off the plants. In fynbos, however, biological factors, while important, play a relatively minor role; instead, four physical influences are the dominant factors in fynbos ecology: summer droughts; low soil nutrients; recurring fires; and constant wind. All four of these factors feature prominently in the Park.

ristea icana

Sugarbush:
Protea repens

Gladiolus:
Geophytes, or bulbous plants like this Gladiolus, are one of the four elements of fynbos.

The 'Father of Fynbos' was Dr Rudolf Marloth (1855-1931), a German analytical chemist who settled in Cape Town and who had a great interest in botany and mountaineering. It was he who first coined the phrase Cape Floral Kingdom to describe the region's floral riches. Marloth made numerous discoveries, including that the Red Disa – the so-called Pride of Table Mountain *(Disa uniflora)* – is pollinated by the Table Mountain Beauty butterfly. His *Flora of South Africa* was published between 1913 and 1932.

CAPE FLORAL KINGDOM: PART III
THE CAPE PENINSULA

If the Cape Floral Kingdom, or fynbos, is a biological treasure chest, then one of its most brilliant gems is the Cape Peninsula. This tiny patch of land, only some 470 sq km in extent, harbours a staggering 2 285 flowering plant species. Botanists never tire of pointing out that

Disa racemosa

the 57 sq km of Table Mountain alone has some 1 470 plant species, only just fewer than the 1 492 found in Britain in an area of 308 000 sq km, and more species than the whole of Sweden, which is a thousand times larger.

Brilliant resident: Malachite Sunbird on the flower of *Mimetes fimbriifolius*

Hidden treasure: Red Disas (*Disa uniflora*) bloom in damp areas.

Rare blossom: *Erica urna-viridis* is found only in the Muizenberg area of the Park.

DELIGHTS IN EVERY SEASON

MOUNTAIN FYNBOS DOMINATES in the Park, although there are at least three other significant vegetation types here as well: remnants of the more fertile Renosterveld on the lower slopes of Lion's Head, Signal Hill and Devil's Peak; Afromontane forest in the kloofs on the cool eastern and southern sides of Table Mountain itself; and tiny patches of Strandveld along the coast. Fynbos is celebrated partly for its high levels of endemism (species occurring naturally nowhere else on earth), and the Cape Peninsula boasts some 90

Featherlight: White everlastings in Silvermine

Linnaeus

Thunberg

Although the indigenous inhabitants knew the many wonderful qualities of fynbos for thousands of years, fynbos also quickly entranced botanists in Europe following the arrival of European explorers at the Cape. As early as 1605, a dried Blue Sugarbush (*Protea neriifolia*) flowerhead was illustrated by Dutch botanist Carolus Clusius. Noted early European botanists who visited the Cape included Swedes Carl Thunberg (1743-1828) – who collected 3 000 specimens in South Africa, 1 000 of which were new to science – and Anders Sparrman (1748-1820). They were both pupils of the renowned Carolus Linnaeus (1707-1778) who devised the taxonomic system of naming all plant and animal species still in use today. Linnaeus formally described many Cape plants sent to him, but personally never visited these shores.

Disa cornuta

Disa ferruginea

Disa nubigena

endemic plant species and at least 112 endemic animals (nearly all invertebrates) – the highest endemism for an area of this size anywhere in the world. By contrast, fewer than 20 of Britain's plants are endemic.

Fynbos contains 526 of the world's 740 ericas, and the Cape Peninsula alone has 112 erica species – the most diverse genus in the Park. In contrast, the whole of Europe has just 14 ericas.

Erica bruniades

The colours of these ericas are exquisite, ranging from blood red to crimson and scarlet to yellow and green. The huge Protea family, with more than 360 species throughout southern Africa, is, appropriately, named after Proteus, the Greek god who had the ability to change himself into numerous forms. More than 90% of this family's southern African representatives are found in the fynbos region – 330 species – and there is not a month when a protea is not in bloom. Of the world's 112 plants in the Protea genus itself – also called the sugarbushes, to avoid confusion with the many other genuses in the Protea family – 69 occur in fynbos. Protea species

Yellow pincushion: *Leucospermum conocarpodendron*

occurring in the Park include the magnificent King Protea (*Protea cynaroides*), which is South Africa's national flower, the Sugarbush (*Protea repens*) and the Black-beard Sugarbush (*Protea lepidocarpodendron*). The lovely Silver Tree (*Leucadendron argenteum*), endemic to the Cape Peninsula, is also a member of the Protea family (▲ 59), as are the Tree Pincushion (*Leucospermum conocarpodendron*) and the Golden Cone Bush (*Leucadendron laureolum*).

Disa tenuifolia

Disa uniflora

Disas for Africa: The many faces of the disa make it one of the delights of the Cape Floral Kingdom. The Park is home to many of the Peninsula's 70-plus species.

Disa fasciata

There are numerous orchid species on the Peninsula, including more than 70 disas, although some of the rarest of these exquisite plants occur on the Cape Flats, outside the Park and other formally protected areas. The disas also range widely in colour, from the bright red of the Pride of Table Mountain (*Disa uniflora*) to yellow, blue, mauve and green.

Although the Cape Peninsula's floral gems are at their most prominent in late winter, spring and early summer, there are botanical delights waiting to entrance the visitor during every month of the year.

Regular sight: An Orange-breasted Sunbird probes an *Erica patersonia* (Mealie Heath).

■ SOME PLANTS OF THE PARK: PART I

Illustrations from Mary Matham Kidd, *Cape Peninsula: South African Wild Flower Guide 3*
Reproduced by kind permission of the Botanical Society of South Africa

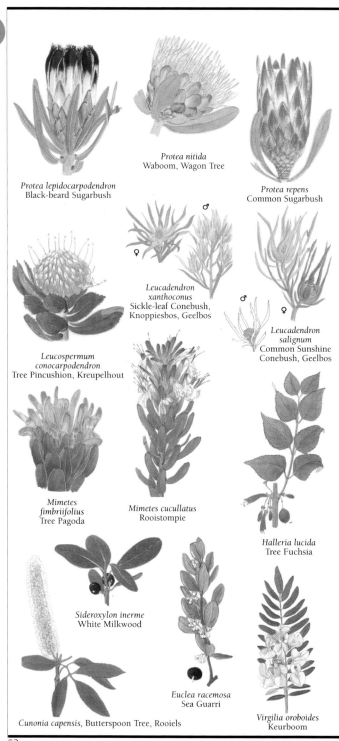

Protea nitida
Waboom, Wagon Tree

Protea lepidocarpodendron
Black-beard Sugarbush

Protea repens
Common Sugarbush

*Leucadendron
xanthoconus*
Sickle-leaf Conebush,
Knoppiesbos, Geelbos

*Leucadendron
salignum*
Common Sunshine
Conebush, Geelbos

*Leucospermum
conocarpodendron*
Tree Pincushion, Kreupelhout

*Mimetes
fimbriifolius*
Tree Pagoda

Mimetes cucullatus
Rooistompie

Halleria lucida
Tree Fuchsia

Sideroxylon inerme
White Milkwood

Euclea racemosa
Sea Guarri

Cunonia capensis, Butterspoon Tree, Rooiels

Virgilia oroboides
Keurboom

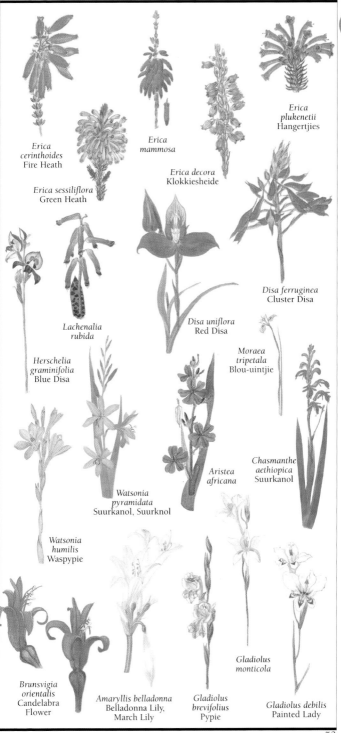

Erica cerinthoides
Fire Heath

Erica sessiliflora
Green Heath

Erica mammosa

Erica decora
Klokkiesheide

Erica plukenetii
Hangertjies

Lachenalia rubida

Herschelia graminifolia
Blue Disa

Disa uniflora
Red Disa

Disa ferruginea
Cluster Disa

Moraea tripetala
Blou-uintjie

Watsonia pyramidata
Suurkanol, Suurknol

Watsonia humilis
Waspypie

Aristea africana

Chasmanthe aethiopica
Suurkanol

Brunsvigia orientalis
Candelabra Flower

Amaryllis belladonna
Belladonna Lily,
March Lily

Gladiolus brevifolius
Pypie

Gladiolus monticola

Gladiolus debilis
Painted Lady

■ SOME PLANTS OF THE PARK: PART II

Illustrations from Mary Matham Kidd, *Cape Peninsula: South African Wild Flower Guide 3*
Reproduced by kind permission of the Botanical Society of South Africa

Oxalis purpurea
Suring

Oxalis eckloniana
Suring

Oxalis dentata
Suring

Gazania pectinata
Botterblom

Dimorphotheca pluvialis
Cape Daisy,
Witbotterblom

Euryops abrotanifolius
Geelmagriet

Osmitopsis asteriscoides
Swamp Daisy

Arctotis acaulis
Gousblom

Empodium plicatum
Autumn Star,
Sterretjie

Cotyledon orbiculata
Varkoor, Honde-Oor

Senecio elegans
Wild Cineraria,
Strandblommetjie

Pelargonium longifolium
Geranium

Pelargonium myrrhifolium
Geranium

Babiana ambigua
Bobbejaantjie

Pelargonium capitatum
Geranium

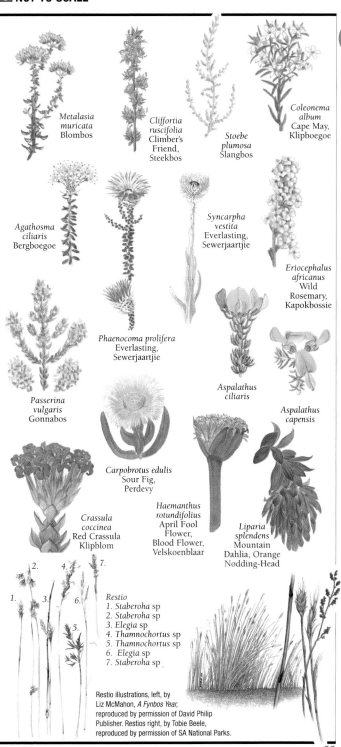

Metalasia muricata
Blombos

Cliffortia ruscifolia
Climber's Friend, Steekbos

Stoebe plumosa
Slangbos

Coleonema album
Cape May, Klipboegoe

Agathosma ciliaris
Bergboegoe

Syncarpha vestita
Everlasting, Sewerjaartjie

Eriocephalus africanus
Wild Rosemary, Kapokbossie

Phaenocoma prolifera
Everlasting, Sewerjaartjie

Aspalathus ciliaris

Aspalathus capensis

Passerina vulgaris
Gonnabos

Carpobrotus edulis
Sour Fig, Perdevy

Crassula coccinea
Red Crassula Klipblom

Haemanthus rotundifolius
April Fool Flower, Blood Flower, Velskoenblaar

Liparia splendens
Mountain Dahlia, Orange Nodding-Head

Restio
1. *Staberoha* sp
2. *Staberoha* sp
3. *Elegia* sp
4. *Thamnochortus* sp
5. *Thamnochortus* sp
6. *Elegia* sp
7. *Staberoha* sp

Restio illustrations, left, by Liz McMahon, *A Fynbos Year*, reproduced by permission of David Philip Publisher. Restios right, by Tobie Beele, reproduced by permission of SA National Parks.

FIRE AND FYNBOS

Fynbos needs fire to survive and flourish. In fact, many of the more than 8 000 fynbos plant species of the Cape Floral Kingdom are totally dependent on fire to germinate and flower. Botanists have discovered that even the smoke from wild fires is a stimulus which sets off the flowering of some fynbos species.

FIRE OF LIFE

Brief glory: The lovely Fire Lily (*Cyrtanthus ventricosus*) only blooms after fire and then remains dormant until the next burn … maybe as much as 30 or even 40 years later.

PUT SIMPLY, WITHOUT FIRE THERE WOULD BE NO FYNBOS. So if you're in the Cape during the summer fire season and see headlines in local newspapers reading "Fynbos destroyed by fire", treat them with scepticism.

Of course, the fire issue is more complex than that, and it's difficult to believe that Nature hasn't suffered a severe trauma when viewing the charred skeletons of plants and animals in the blackened, dusty wasteland that is the aftermath of most fires in the Park. But, mostly, fires that occur naturally – started principally by lightning strikes, but also possibly by sparks from rocks dislodged in landslides or by foraging baboons – and at reasonably long intervals, are highly beneficial for fynbos.

It was only in the 1960s that botanists and plant ecologists began to understand the complex relationship between fynbos and fire.

Over millennia, fynbos plants developed four main strategies to survive fire and even to use it to advantage: having seeds which rodents or ants store underground for food (▲ 67, 75); through regeneration from underground bulbs or corms – like watsonias which erupt in massive colourful displays after fire; resprouting from woody rootstocks, such as the King Protea (*Protea cynaroides*); and having dormant buds deep within the stem, protected from fire by thick bark, like the Waboom (*Protea nitida*).

HOW OFTEN SHOULD FIRES OCCUR?

Ecologists refer to a "fire regime" with four major components: frequency – how often fires occur; season – the time of year of fires relative to the plants' reproductive cycle; fire intensity – the fire's temperature ("hotter" or "cooler") which depends mainly on fuel load; and size – over what area the fire burns. It is the fire regime of an area that determines how beneficial, or how damaging, fire is. For

example, too frequent fires can radically alter the species mix of an area, and cause local extinctions of some plants.

Many fynbos plant species benefit from a fire regime of relatively "cool" fires in late summer or early autumn (February, March and April) and at intervals of about 12 to 15 years. Unseasonal and accidental fires can harm fynbos.

■ Please take special care to avoid starting fires, and report immediately any fires that you see.

Above: This section of the Park at Silvermine appears devastated by fire.
Below: An area of mature fynbos near Cape Point which looked just like the landscape above after a fire 14 years ago.

■ FORESTS

African Olive-Pigeon (Rameron Pigeon)

Olive Thrush

LIFE IN THE SHADE

Protected: Permits are needed to enter Orange Kloof forest.

SOME FUNGI OF PARK FORESTS

Bracket fungi

Chicken of the woods

Fly agaric

Clathrus archeri

Playing its part: Mist helps maintain the forest's cool, moist conditions.

AFROMONTANE FOREST, as its name implies, describes the forest associated with the mountains of Africa, and is found in patches throughout the continent. Generally, Afromontane forest is found below an altitude of 1 000m and, in the south, it can grow close to sea level (as on the Peninsula). Usually found in kloofs (canyons) or on cool, south- and south-east-facing slopes, this forest type requires at least 800mm of rain annually, supplemented by mist. It is of medium to tall height (15m to 30m), evergreen, and grows on reasonably nutrient-rich soils that have good water-retention. It is dominated by a relatively small number of trees like the Rooiels (*Cunonia capensis*), Assegaai Tree (*Curtisia dentata*), Bastard Saffronwood (*Cassine peragua*), Ironwood (*Olea capensis*), Hard Pear (*Olinia ventosa*), Cape Beech (*Rapanea melanophloeos*), Cape Holly (*Ilex mitis*), Stinkwood (*Ocotea bullata*) and, of course, the Real Yellowwood (*Podocarpus latifolius*). Some 10 to 20 species are common to all Afromontane forest which does not boast high species diversity. This forest does not support large numbers of vertebrate animals, and the fruits of its trees are dispersed mainly by birds. Because its foliage has a low flammability, most fires are only able to singe the forest margins, leaving the heart intact. This is why there is usually a relatively abrupt transition between the forest and adjoining fire-prone fynbos.

Cape Robin-Chat

THERE IS NO RECORD OF THE SIZE of the indigenous forests on the Cape Peninsula before the arrival of the European colonists. Presumably they were more extensive – particularly in a place like Hout Bay, which was named for its trees – but the forest habitat would always have been restricted by the nature of the Peninsula's geography, and the mountainside would not have been covered in a continuous forest belt, as is often presumed. The indigenous Khoekhoen and San probably had only a minimal impact on the forests, through their use of fire – affecting mainly the forest margins – and the harvesting of saplings for poles and assegaais (spears).

Rolling in: Morning mist brings moisture to Newlands forest.

But the arrival of the settlers changed all that. The new colonial society was totally wood-dependent; and it has been estimated that within just 50 to 70 years of the arrival of the first Europeans, local indigenous forests had been decimated. Subsequent land use practices, including agriculture and afforestation, worsened the problem. Today, the only substantial patches of indigenous forest are along the cool, moist eastern slopes and in the ravines of Table Mountain, between Kirstenbosch and Devil's Peak (▲110/13); in two small areas above Kalk Bay (▲ 126/7); in Orange Kloof above Hout Bay – the largest remaining Afromontane forest segment in the Park – and below

Egyptian Fruit Bat

Old Man's Beard

Chapman's Peak. In coastal forest patches close to the sea – like at Llandudno – the White Milkwood (*Sideroxylon inerme*) dominates, but most of these patches have been devastated by development.
In the Park, 33 species of forest tree have been recorded. Because of the dense shade under the forest canopy, only a few other plants are able to grow. The most common species are ferns, particularly those of the genus *Blechnum* and the Sword Sedge *Schoenoxiphium lanceum*. In this dark shade, rocks and boulders are soon covered with the lesser plants: mosses and liverworts.
The cool, moist, nutrient-rich forest floor abounds with life, although not many of the large and spectacular variety. Mites, insect larvae, springtails, centipedes, millipedes, dung beetles, earthworms, mountain cockroaches, stick insects, woodlice, slugs, harvestmen, sowbugs and amphipods are among the invertebrates which occur here – many of them endemic – and which all play a very important role in the forest ecology.

A CAPE SPECIAL

The lovely Silver Tree (*Leucadendron argenteum*) is endemic to the Cape Peninsula, probably occurring naturally only on Lion's Head and in the Wynberg Hill-Kirstenbosch area on heavy gravel soils derived from Malmesbury shales and granite. It is a member of the protea family and one of the few 'tree proteas', usually growing to a height of 5 to 7m but it can reach 16m. Silver Trees are flowering plants, but their flower heads, or inflorescences, look like cones. They are dioecious: the sexes are on separate trees. Their silvery, shimmering sheen is derived from the fine, silky, silver-coloured hairs which densely cover the leaves and help prevent them from desiccating (drying out) in the hot summer sun. Seeds, which have four silky plumes, are wind-dispersed, but birds help because they use the seeds as nesting material. Silver Trees were extensive in areas of their preferred soil type, but huge stands were devastated by clearing for agriculture and through fire after the arrival of the colonial settlers.

■ RIVERS AND WETLANDS

Magnificent sight: The African Fish-Eagle (*Haliaeetus vocifer*) can be seen near the Noordhoek/Kommetjie wetlands.

It was probably the presence of sweet, perennial water flowing off Table Mountain that first attracted humans to the Cape Peninsula, and it was certainly these streams – which turn into small but powerful rivers during the rainy season in winter – that allowed the "Tavern of the Seas" at the base of the mountain to develop and thrive.

FROM TRICKLES TO TORRENTS

THE PARK'S MAJOR PERENNIAL rivers, which are little more than streams in high summer, are the Liesbeek, created by several tributaries flowing down the gorges of the eastern slopes of Table Mountain and converging at Kirstenbosch, and the Disa, which drains the Back Table area of Table Mountain and flows south into Hout Bay.

The Silvermine River rises in the Steenberg mountains and flows east into False Bay. In the far south of the Peninsula, the Klaasjagers River rises in the Swartkop mountains, flows west along the boundary of the Cape of Good Hope section of the Park and then into the Park where it is joined by the Houte stream to become the Kromme River with an important estuary at Die Mond on the West coast. These are all typical fynbos rivers characterised by a golden amber colour which becomes darker brown or even black where the water is deeper – fynbos waterbodies are generally known as "blackwater lakelets". This colouration is caused by chemicals – humic acids or polyphenols – originating as a defence mechanism in fynbos plants to discourage grazing (the simplest phenol is carbolic acid). When the plants die, the chemicals are leached back into the soil and groundwater, and from there into the streams and vleis. So not only is the water coloured, but it also becomes slightly acidic, which limits the number of plants and animals able to survive in it. There is only one indigenous fish species in the Park's rivers: the small, near-transparent Cape Galaxias (*Galaxias zebratus*). There are at least 17 frog species, including the common Cape River Frog (*Afrana fuscigula*) and the Banded Stream Frog (*Strongylopus bonaspei*). The freshwater River Crab (*Potamonautes perlatus*), is the largest invertebrate in the streams.

▮ ALIEN THREAT

The alien Mallard duck (*Anas platyrhynchos*) is a major problem because it hybridises freely with the indigenous Yellow-billed Duck (*Anas undulata*), above, threatening the latter's genetic integrity.

A SERIOUSLY ENDANGERED INHABITANT

Common Platanna

Cape Platanna

Cape Galaxias

One of the Park's most important animals is the Cape Platanna *(Xenopus gilli)*, which is among the world's most endangered amphibians. Only discovered in the 1920s, it lives exclusively in the acidic blackwater pools associated with fynbos, where it survives despite these pools sometimes drying out in summer. In the Park, *X. gilli* is found only in the Cape of Good Hope section. Unfortunately the provision of permanent water holes and dams here allowed colonisation by its bigger 'cousin', the Common Platanna (*X. laevis*), which was introduced from Rondevlei. The more aggressive common frog both hybridises with and cannibalises the diminutive endangered platanna, threatening its survival. Park staff are helping herpetologists devise a management plan to care for the Cape Platanna.

Important estuary: The Kromme River meets the ocean at Die Mond

Precious: The newly-cleared Noordhoek-Kommetjie wetlands.

WHAT IS A WETLAND?

Wetlands encompass many kinds of water bodies, ranging from pools that develop during the rainy season but become dry grassy depressions for the rest of the year, to the extreme case of stretches of river bank that may only flood a couple of times a century. The usual definition of a wetland, therefore, is a region in which the soils show signs of waterlogging. These soils tend to be grey or black, and often have a characteristic 'muddy' smell.

WETLAND JEWELS

River Crab

HISTORICALLY, MUCH OF THE CAPE FLATS was a wetland, and although large areas still flood every winter, most of the functional wetland system has disappeared under extensive urban development, remaining only in conserved areas like Rondevlei Nature Reserve (▲ 158/9). The Noordhoek-Kommetjie wetlands are the most extensive in the Park by far, and constitute one of its ecological jewels. This area was in private ownership for many years, when it was severely neglected. Dense stands of invasive alien vegetation took root and the wetlands were negatively affected by the increasingly polluted, and growing volumes of, run-off from the rapidly expanding urban development in the Noordhoek valley. That changed when 450ha forming the heart of these wetlands were acquired by the Park in 2002, thanks to a number of generous funders. This area is extremely important for conservation: not only because of the special wetland plant and animal communities which inhabit it, but because it forms the only remaining natural link between the southern and northern sections of the Park, creating a biological corridor for plant and animal migration.

Much of the Central Table area on the top of Table Mountain near Maclear's Beacon is a wetland area, fed during the summer by moisture condensed from the south-easterly wind's "Table Cloth" clouds. This area drains slowly down the steep, south-facing slopes of the Back Table, in places like Echo Valley, where the moist cliffs are home to a unique group of plants and animals. These include summer-flowering orchids like the Drip Disa (*Disa longicornis*), *Disa rosea*, *Disa richardiana* and *Disa maculata*. Other wetland areas in the Park host some of the Peninsula's rarest plants, including the beautiful Bokmakieriestert (*Witsenia maura*, ▲ 24), *Erica heleogena* – its species name means "born from the marsh" – which occurs only in the Klawer Vlei on Red Hill, and three endemic Leucadendrons, or conebushes, all associated with wetland seeps or damp cliffs and all in the Red Data Book of endangered species.

Blacksmith Lapwing (Plover)

Cape Chirping Frog (Moss Frog)

Cape Longclaw chicks

Typical animal species in wetland areas include the Cape Clawless Otter (*Aonyx capensis*), Water Mongoose (*Atilax paludinosus*), Vlei Rat (*Otomys irroratus*) and the tiny Cape Chirping Frog (*Arthroleptella lightfooti*) – one of only two endemic vertebrate species in the Park (the other is the Table Mountain Ghost Frog, (▲ 73). Birds include the Blacksmith Lapwing (*Vanellus armatus*), Levaillant's Cisticola (*Cisticola tinniens*) – in Afrikaans, the "vleitinktinkie", describing its habitat and call – and the striking Cape Longclaw (*Macronyx capensis*).

Vlei Rat

ALIEN INVASIVES: PART I

Hakea sericea

High altitude: An 'alien buster' on the Table Mountain cliffs.

A MASSIVE THREAT TO BIODIVERSITY

ALL OVER THE WORLD, invasive alien plant and animal species are wreaking ecological havoc and exacting huge economic costs, and the Park is unfortunately no exception. Invasive alien plants probably constitute one of the two biggest threats to the effective conservation of the Park's globally important biological diversity; the other is human encroachment through continual development into the Peninsula's remaining natural areas. The habitats of at least 63 endemic and threatened indigenous plants have been densely invaded by alien plants, and they face a real risk of extinction unless these alien species are removed.

Although a handful of alien species had been introduced to the Cape as long as several thousand years ago, for example the Khoekhoe pastoralists' sheep, it was only after the arrival of the European colonists in the mid-17th century that the real problems started. Many alien plants species were introduced, and of these, several proved to be aggressively invasive and severely damaging to the rich natural flora.

Because of the insatiable demand for wood by both the colonists and the crews of passing

THE EFFECTS OF INVASIVE ALIEN SPECIES

THEY INCREASE:

- Erosion
- Fire risk
- Cost of land management

THEY REDUCE:

- Biodiversity
- Number of rare and threatened plants
- Water yield
- Medicinal plant potential
- Agricultural potential
- Ecotourism potential

Long-leaved Wattle with wasp galls.

Wasteland: Fire through a dense stand of Myrtle above Fish Hoek leaves devastation.

ships, local timber was quickly exhausted, and soon serious efforts were made to grow foreign trees. The Cluster Pine (*Pinus pinaster*) – one of the worst alien invasives – was introduced from the Mediterranean region as early as about 1680, and other species introduced early in the Cape's history included two other pines – the Stone Pine (*P. pinea*) and the Aleppo Pine (*P. halepensis*) – the European oak, poplars and the first of three hakea species: the Rock Hakea (*Hakea gibbosa*). The other two hakeas which arrived later were the Silky Hakea (*H. sericea*) and Sweet Hakea (*H. suaveolens*) – all three are Australian members of the Protea family.

Major cost: Dealing with alien-fuelled fires is expensive.

BRINGING ALIENS UNDER CONTROL

There are three main methods of invasive alien plant control:
- mechanical (cutting with loppers, slashers or chain saws; hand-pulling; burning);
- chemical control (blanket-spraying, spot-spraying or the focused application of herbicides); and
- biological control (the use of biocontrol agents).

BIOCONTROL is a particularly effective long-term control measure; although it will never totally eradicate an alien species, it can reduce population levels to such an extent that other control measures are no longer a major drain on management budgets.

Gall rust

A highly effective and unusual biocontrol agent released on the Peninsula is the Western Australian Gall Rust *Uromycladium tepperianum*, (see right). It has infected many adult Port Jackson plants, creating galls which reduce seed production and vigour, until the heavily galled plants eventually die.

Other biocontrol agents include seed-eaters which attack Hakea, Blackwood, Stinkbean and Black Wattle; a bud-galling wasp which reduces seed production in Long-leaved Wattle (see right; leaf, flower and pod feeders for Sesbania; fungi which reduce vigour in Hakea and Port Jackson; and moth larvae which destroy fruits (Hakea).

Galls on a Long-leaved Wattle caused by the wasp.

Alien invaders: From left, Pine, Hakea, Rooikrans (*Acacia cyclops*) and Blackwood. 63

In January 2000, devastating wildfires – fuelled by dense stands of invasive alien vegetation – swept through the southern Peninsula for nearly a week, causing major ecological damage and destroying property. Determined to prevent a similar disaster from ever happening again, a unique public-private partnership was created: the Ukuvuka-Operation Firestop campaign (*Ukuvuka* is a Xhosa word meaning 'Wake up'), which aimed to rid the Peninsula of alien invasive plants, rehabilitate fire-damaged areas, and fire-proof vulnerable communities. The founding sponsors were the Cape Argus newspaper and Santam insurance company. Other major sponsors were Nedbank's Green Trust, Total, City of Cape Town and the Working for Water Programme of the Department of Water Affairs and Forestry. The four-year campaign started in June 2000, and had a budget of about R70-million, much of which was spent in the Park.

■ ALIEN INVASIVES: PART II

THE CAPE'S ALIEN NIGHTMARE

IN 1830, BARON VON LUDWIG established a garden in Cape Town where he planted 1 660 plants from all over the world. His one-time curator was J Bowie, a botanist who imported the seeds of several Australian Acacias; these were to become the Cape's worst invaders. Bowie later took over a section of the Government Garden to grow "useful" exotics, including Eucalyptus, Hakea, Casuarina and *Acacia melanoxylon* (Blackwood), also from Australia. Others also imported alien plants, which soon spread into the natural veld by wind, birds and humans. This was particularly the case on the Cape Flats, which by the mid 19th-century had been virtually denuded of vegetation through the collection of firewood, restios (reeds) for thatching, fuel for lime kilns, and grazing by domestic animals. This exposed the sandy soils and led to serious wind-blown driftsand problems on the roads and railway line. The government responded by planting numerous alien trees to act as windbreaks and to stabilise the loose sand, including Port Jackson Willow (*A. saligna*); a "New South Wales shrub" (*A. cyclops*) which soon became known by its Afrikaans name, Rooikrans, meaning red seed stalk; various gum species; Myrtle (*Leptospermum laevigatum*); poplars; and other pine trees, including the Californian Pine (*Pinus radiata*). Although the Cape Flats bore the brunt of the aliens, the impact on Table Mountain was almost as bad. Here, big stands of Cluster Pine (*P. pinaster*), Stone Pine (*P. pinea*) and Blackwood were cultivated, as well as oaks, poplars and eucalypts. Because of the barren and devastated appearance of the mountain – partly as a result of the frequent fires, partly because of the endless demand for firewood – there was a growing public clamour for a greening initiative, and in the 1880s an aggressive afforestation programme was launched. Unfortunately it was again the Cluster Pine that dominated; even members of the Mountain Club were encouraged to scatter its seed during their rambles.

Protecting the soil: (left) Gabions are installed after a fire to prevent soil run-off in an area damaged by alien plants.

Marine invader: The European Mussel is harvested as a favourite Cape delicacy, but it has displaced indigenous mussels.

FURTHER PLANTING OF ALIEN SPECIES occurred on Devil's Peak and at Hout Bay, Silvermine and Tokai. There was even a memorial erected to forester Frank Jarman, who was responsible for the Devil's Peak plantations, following his death in 1905. It reads: "He found these barren stony slopes treeless and left them covered with forest." Ironic words in today's more enlightened world! Some botanists appreciated the real threat posed by the invasive alien plants, and particularly the Cluster Pines. They included Dr Rudolf Marloth (▲49), then Mountain Club of SA president, and his pupil, General Smuts, who railed in a letter about "these useless horrid pines, the planting of which in the Peninsula has been a calamity".

The first warnings went unheeded, but gradually enthusiasm for indigenous plants grew. In 1938 all three Hakea species were declared noxious weeds, and, following a warning in 1945 by the Royal Society, the first Cluster Pine removals started. Alien clearing started in the Cape of Good Hope section of the Park in the early 1960s, and there were similar efforts in the Table Mountain and Silvermine nature reserves after their proclamation, also in the '60s, but without enough funds to ever do the job properly in these two areas. Finally, in the 1990s – mainly following the proclamation of the Park, but also through supporting initiatives like the Working for Water programme and Ukuvuka-Operation Firestop – a firm commitment was made to rid the Peninsula's natural areas of the scourge of invasive plants.

ALIEN ANIMALS ARE ALSO PART OF THE PARK'S MANAGEMENT PROBLEMS

Cecil John Rhodes is rightly blamed for causing several environmental problems, but one he was not responsible for was the introduction of the alien Himalayan Tahr *(Hemitragus jemlahicus)*. This species, related to the goat, occurs naturally in the mountainous regions of India and Nepal, where its status is 'threatened'. In 1936, a pair escaped from Groote Schuur Zoo on the slopes of Devil's Peak (since closed), made their way up the mountain and became the nucleus of a herd that numbered at least 600 in 1976. Tahr cause substantial ecological damage, particularly in recently burnt areas, and a culling programme before the Park was established reduced numbers to about 100. The Park is committed to removing the tahr and a new culling programme was initiated in 1999. This was temporarily stopped through legal action by the Friends of the Tahr group which opposed the culling. This legal dispute was due to be resolved in 2004. Other alien mammals due to be removed are the Sambar *(Cervus unicolour)*, from Newlands Forest, and the Fallow Deer *(Cervus dama)* from Rhodes Estate.

■ MAMMALS OF THE PARK

I **SUN-SEEKERS**
The Rock
Dassie (*Procavia capensis*) or Rock
Hyrax occurs
widely in the sub-region and can
almost always be
seen at the Upper
Cableway Station
on sunny days.
Dassies are
diurnal, only
emerging from
rocky crevices
once the sun is up
and returning
before sunset.
They are
herbivores and
thrive in areas of
nutrient-poor,
unpalatable plant
species scorned
by other grazers.
The Dassie is so
unlike other
animals that it has
its own order
(*Hyracoidea*) all to
itself. It is the
elephant's nearest
living relative, but
not due to any
easily observed
similarities.
Rather, it is
because hyraxes,
elephants and sea
cows (dugongs
and manatees) all
descended from a
common ancestor
millions of years
ago. The three
modern groups
still share some
physiological
similarities in
teeth, leg and foot
bones, and have
testes that do not
descend into a
scrotum. The
Dassie's name
derives from the
Dutch word for
badger: *dasje*.

The indigenous inhabitants of the Cape Peninsula would have known all the local animals intimately,

Handsome: Mountain Zebra at Cape Point.

given their hunter-gatherer and pastoralist lifestyles, but unfortunately no record of that relationship has survived.

IN THE FIRING LINE OF THE SETTLERS

THE EVOCATIVE ROCK ART of the San (Bushmen) that adorns shelters in many other parts of the sub-continent and depicts animals like the Eland (*Taurotragus oryx*) and African Elephant (*Loxodonta africana*) in strikingly accurate detail, is sadly absent from the Park.
The first written records of animals in the region are from the passing European sailors who wrote particularly about the "wild deer" or "antelope" they saw on the

Shy local: The tiny Grysbok is a fynbos endemic, lying up during the day in cover.

shores. Historically, Lion (*Panthera leo*) and Leopard (*P. pardus*) – the latter called "tigers" in the early days – occurred. Jan van Riebeeck, the first Dutch commander, complained regularly about the frequent predations by Lion on stock, and instituted a bounty reward system for Lion, Leopard and Hyena – probably the Spotted Hyena (*Crocuta crocuta*). There is no firm date for the killing of the last Lion on the Peninsula but it was probably in the 1720s. The Leopard survived locally into the 19th century.
In his diaries, Van Riebeeck makes no mention of Zebra (*Equus* spp), Elephant or Buffalo on the Peninsula. The closest any historical report puts elephants to

FEW ANIMALS IN FYNBOS

Most fynbos soils
are sandy,
coarse-grained,
acidic and very
low in nutrients.
This is why
fynbos makes for
very poor grazing
and has
historically
supported few
big game species
and low
concentrations of
smaller game.
Where large
grazers and
browsers did
occur – like
Eland and Black
Rhinoceros –
they would have
concentrated on
the adjoining
renosterveld
vegetation
growing on fertile
shale soils, or
among the
coastal plants on
the deep, well-drained sands
supporting
strandveld
vegetation, rather
than in fynbos
itself.

The secretive and the show-off: The timid Steenbok, top, and the Bontebok. The latter is often seen in the Cape Point area.

the Peninsula is at Tiervlei – about 10km north-east of the city – in 1702, but these animals were in the region, for the Khoekhoen wore ivory bracelets and traded tusks. The Black Rhinoceros (*Diceros bicornis*) appears to have been restricted to the Cape Flats. Two Zebra species – the now extinct Quagga (*Equus quagga quagga*) (▲33) and the Mountain Zebra (*E. zebra zebra*) – appear to have occurred close to the Peninsula, but possibly not on it. Two big mammals which almost certainly occurred here were the Eland and, in the flatter areas, the Red Hartebeest (*Alcelaphus buselaphus*). The Hippopotamus (*Hippopotamus amphibius*) was found in vleis and wetlands on the Cape Flats. It was quickly shot out, but has since been reintroduced to Rondevlei (▲158/9). Today, big game is restricted to the fenced Cape of Good Hope section of the Park; here there are Eland, Red Hartebeest, Mountain Zebra, Grey Rhebok (*Pelea capreolus*), Bontebok (*Damaliscus dorcas dorcas*) and Klipspringer (▲136). A small antelope found throughout the Park is the Grysbok (*Raphicerus melanotis*) – a fynbos endemic – while Steenbok (*Raphicerus campestris*) and Duiker (*Sylvicapra grimmia*) occur in small numbers. Widespread but not often seen are the Cape Clawless Otter (*Aonyx capensis*), Large-spotted Genet (*Genetta tigrina*), Small-spotted Genet (*G. genetta*), Water Mongoose (*Atilax paludinosus*), Striped Polecat (*Ictonyx striatus*) and the biggest remaining predator, the Caracal or Lynx (*Felis caracal*). The Cape Silver Fox (*Vulpes chama*) was reintroduced to the Cape Point area and now occurs as far north as Newlands Forest. The Small Grey Mongoose (*Galerella purverulenta*) is often seen and the Porcupine (*Hystrix africaeaustralis*, left) is a common raider of gardens on the Park's borders. Unmistakable if seen emerging from its massive sandy burrow is the endemic Cape Dune Molerat (*Bathyergus suillus*) which digs with its huge, chisel-like front teeth.

Nocturnal: The Cape Gerbil (*Tatera afra*).

Seed eater: The Striped Mouse (*Rhabdomys pumilio*).

Agent: The Cape Spiny Mouse (*Acomys subspinosus*) aids protea pollination.

HELPERS OF THE FYNBOS

At least 20 different Protea plants are believed to be pollinated by various mouse species. This astounding discovery, made in the late 1970s, caused a major stir in the botanical community. Unlike their more showy cousins, the ground-flowering proteas do not have bright flowerheads. Instead, the dull flowers have a strong yeasty odour that attracts the nocturnal rodents and allows them to locate the protea's rich nectar in the dark. The rodents feed on this by thrusting their heads into the flowers, becoming dusted with pollen which they then transfer to other plants.

■ BABOONS

Hierarchy: Grooming is a very important social activity.

A favourite food: The fruit of the Sour Fig (*Carpobrotus edulis*) which grows abundantly on dunes in the Park.

Baboon-watching features highly on the "must do" list of many visitors to the Park, and with good reason. Baboons are wonderfully entertaining to watch, engaging in much socially recognisable behaviour that reminds us that we humans are also primates, and showing off their obvious intelligence and marvellous physical strength and agility. Unfortunately, many people forget that baboons are wild animals and need to be treated as such.

WILD AT HEART, DESPITE THEIR APPEAL

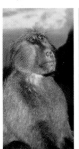

ⓘ HOW YOU CAN HELP

Baboons regularly get injured. These can be natural injuries, such as when mature males fight with each other, inflicting deep slashes with their large canines, or unnatural – for example, when they are struck by vehicles or shot or stoned by aggressive humans.

If you see a seriously injured baboon anywhere in the Peninsula, please report it as soon as possible to one of the following:

■ Park authorities
☎ (021) 780-9100
■ Kommetjie Environmental Awareness Group,
☎ (021) 783-3433
■ City of Cape Town's nature conservation department,
☎ (021) 715-8081

Family group: Baboons seem so human it's easy to forget they are wild animals.

CHACMA BABOONS (*Papio ursinus*) evolved from an ancestral baboon prototype some 1.5 million years ago, and are believed to be the oldest of the five species (some say sub-species) of baboons in Africa. They occur widely in the sub-region of southern Africa, except in desert areas, and are not threatened as a species, although their numbers are declining. But on the Peninsula, where they may have been living for as long as one million years, they are critically endangered.

With the arrival of European settlers and the growth of metropolitan Cape Town across the Cape Flats, the local animals have been effectively cut off from baboon troops elsewhere in the Western Cape. As their numbers dwindle through conflict with the increasing human population, there is no natural recruitment from outside. Also, as urban areas have spread over the years, the natural area available to the baboons has been steadily reduced. Partly for these reasons, and partly because the highly intelligent baboons have come to identify residential areas with easy food sources – for example, fruit trees in gardens, unsecured rubbish bins or pet food – most local baboons now engage in "raiding" at least some of the time.

At present (2004), there are about 360 baboons left on the Cape Peninsula living in 10 troops, but none occurs on Table Mountain north of Constantia Nek. The most northerly troop lives around Tokai, Constantiaberg and Silvermine, ➤

Awesome: Baboons have huge canines.

SAFETY FIRST

Although baboons will not attack people and are generally not dangerous, some have become very aggressive in their search for food and will enter cars or snatch bags, packets or food like ice-creams and chips. The situation may become dangerous, depending on how you handle it. The general rule is to remain calm – don't panic or scream, and NEVER try to grab back something from a baboon. Once a baboon has food, or thinks it has food, it will fight to keep it. Male baboons in particular are very strong and have huge canines, and all baboons can bite and scratch. A baboon will probably eventually drop anything that isn't food and this can be retrieved later. Keep car windows shut when baboons are around, and pack away securely any food if you're picnicking. Baboons are adept at reading body-language: be confident and serious when chasing them away.
Never look a baboon directly in the eye as this constitutes a challenge.

Why do some baboons have pink bottoms? As part of their reproductive cycle, all mature female baboons experience a swelling of the sexual skin on their buttocks. This occurs over 10 days, and when the swelling is biggest and brightest, ovulation occurs. This is when the male baboons compete most actively to copulate with the female. In the seven days after ovulation, her pink skin deflates.

SLOWLY DOES IT

Please **SLOW DOWN** when you see baboons on the road! Although they are very smart animals in many ways, baboons do not understand that cars are dangerous, nor do they know what hooters mean. The baboons are attracted to roads because of the warm surfaces and the presence of food like squashed insects. They have also learned that some 'cars' provide food – illegally!

Watchful: Baboon monitors keep an eye on their charges.

➤ and the others are all in the southern Peninsula. Five troops are mostly, but not entirely, confined to the fenced Cape of Good Hope section of the Park. The only troop which does not raid human settlements is the tiny Klein Olifantsbos troop on the Atlantic coastline near Cape Point. Previously, any "problem" baboons were simply shot. Now, a more enlightened management approach has been adopted. A Baboon Management Team, comprising conservation officers, scientists, municipal officials and local community groups, has been set up to try to reduce baboon-human conflict. This team employs "baboon monitors": full-time employees who follow the baboons throughout the day and attempt to keep them out of residential areas like Da Gama Park, Kommetjie and Scarborough. These monitors have been highly successful in reducing the number of raids and hence conflict with humans, but there have not been enough funds to employ monitors to watch all the troops outside the Park.

SOME MAMMALS OF THE PARK

Illustrations by Clare Abbott
from *Land Mammals of South Africa. A field guide*
by Reay HN Smithers
Reproduced by kind permission of Hazel Smithers

Cape Molerat
(*Georhycus capensis*)

Chacma baboon
(*Papio ursinus*)

Striped Mouse
(*Rhabdomys pumilio*)

Porcupine
(*Hystrix africaeaustralis*)

Cape Dune Molerat
(*Bathyergus suillus*)

Striped Polecat
(*Ictonyx striatus*)

Rock Dassie
(*Procavia capensis*)

Vlei Rat
(*Otomys irroratus*)

Small Grey Mongoose
(*Galerella purverulenta*)

Small-spotted Genet
(*Genetta genetta*)

Large-spotted Genet
(*Genetta tigrina*)

Cape Clawless Otter
(*Aonyx capensis*)

Water Mongoose
(*Atilax paludinosus*)

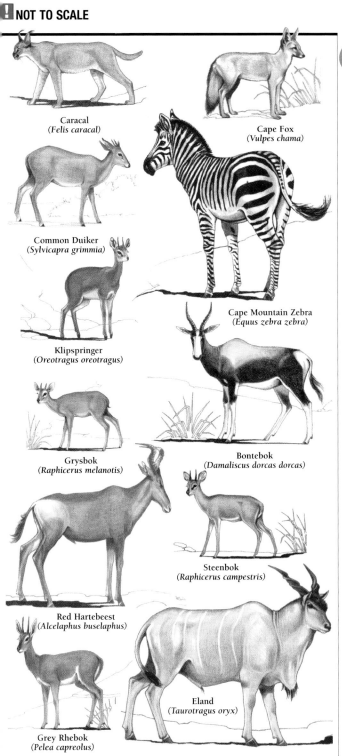

Caracal
(*Felis caracal*)

Cape Fox
(*Vulpes chama*)

Common Duiker
(*Sylvicapra grimmia*)

Klipspringer
(*Oreotragus oreotragus*)

Cape Mountain Zebra
(*Equus zebra zebra*)

Grysbok
(*Raphicerus melanotis*)

Bontebok
(*Damaliscus dorcas dorcas*)

Steenbok
(*Raphicerus campestris*)

Red Hartebeest
(*Alcelaphus buselaphus*)

Grey Rhebok
(*Pelea capreolus*)

Eland
(*Taurotragus oryx*)

■ REPTILES & AMPHIBIANS

Quick draw: A Cape Dwarf Chameleon (*Bradypodion pumilum*), endemic to the fynbos region, captures its prey with its tongue.

Some slither, others scuttle and several bask in the sun, disinclined to move unless they really have to. A few amble slowly through the veld, or sit quietly on the banks of the pools, ready to plop into the water at the first sign of danger. These are the reptiles and amphibians of the Park, a diverse and fascinating group that complement the unique plant life.

ALL PUFFED UP

One of the oddest, and ugliest, amphibians in the Park is the fynbos endemic Cape Rain Frog (*Breviceps gibbosus*), also known by its Afrikaans name Blaasop – literally, 'blow up'. It's an unlikely frog in that it is quite unable to swim and is totally averse to water. If one lands in a pool, it will blow itself up like a puff-ball and drift ashore on the wind. This curious species, common on the mountain's lower slopes and in suburban gardens, lives in underground chambers in soft loamy soil, emerging only to mate after winter rain. The tadpoles form and metamorphose in jelly-like capsules in the soil, and emerge as fully-formed frogs. A similar species, the Mountain Rain Frog (*Breviceps montanus*), occurs higher on the mountain.

THE WEIRD AND THE WONDERFUL

THE REPTILES MOST VISITORS are likely to encounter are the Southern Rock Agama (*Agama atra* ▲ 102) and the Black Girdled Lizard (*Cordylus niger* ▲77). The browny-grey agama is commonly called by its Afrikaans name Koggelmander, which derives from the male's habit of bobbing up and down rapidly on its front legs during the mating season, when it also develops a bright blue-green head. The lizard, nicknamed the "Cape crocodile", is all black, and its beautifully sculpted scales give it a prehistoric look. Both species feed on insects. Another lizard commonly seen sunning itself on rocks, is the Cape Skink (*Mabuya capensis*).

Master of disguise: A Puff Adder is difficult to see in fynbos. It is one of 22 snake species in the Park: 10 of them non-venomous, 7 mildly venomous and 5 highly venomous – the Puff Adder, Cape Cobra, Berg Adder, Rinkhals and Boomslang.

Visitors, especially to Cape Point, are very likely to see the Angulate Tortoise (*Chersina angulata*), particularly in spring and summer. This species is very vulnerable to fire, so it is more often found in Strandveld vegetation closer to the coast or in Renosterveld – these plant communities are both more palatable and less likely to burn than mountain fynbos. Another tortoise species is the small Common Padloper ("road walker") or Parrot-beaked Tortoise (*Homopus areolatus*), which finds shelter in rodent burrows during fires. Both tortoise species lay their eggs about five centimetres below the soil surface, so that they

Cape Cobra: Lightning fast if it strikes but actually shy, it will keep out of the way of people if it can.

Cape Rain Frog

Young adventurer: A newly hatched Angulate Tortoise.

survive low-intensity fires. Terrapins (*Pelomedusa subrufa*) are found in some waterbodies in the Park. Approach a stream or pond and you're bound to hear a frog "plop" into the water: probably the Cape River Frog (*Afrana fuscigula*), a strong swimmer that lives wherever there's open water. There are at least 17 species of frogs and toads in the Park, ranging from the tiny Arum Lily Frog (*Hyperolius horstocki*) to the hefty Western Leopard Toad (*Bufo pantherinus*), also known as the Snoring or August Toad – both names are from its mating habits. The extremely rare Table Mountain Ghost Frog (*Heleophryne rosei*) – formerly known as the Thumbed Ghost Frog – is one of the Park's natural wonders, and one of only two of its vertebrate endemics. The other is also a frog: the diminutive Cape Chirping Frog (Moss Frog, *Arthroleptella lightfooti*). The Ghost Frog has evolved in isolation for millions of years since Table Mountain became separated from the rest of the Cape Fold Mountains, and it occurs only in seven fast-flowing mountain streams. It is nocturnal, completely silent and very secretive. These frogs have strong clubbed fingertips with adhesive pads which help them grip in the tough conditions, and their tadpoles have large suction discs around their mouths which they use to stay anchored to rocks as they feed on algae, fungi and bacteria.

Rare sight: Table Mountain Ghost Frog

Harmless: Mole Snake

Sleek: Cape Skink

☠ **SNAKES ALIVE!**
Most snakes are shy and retiring, and will try to avoid all human contact. But they will resort to some intimidation or warning – particularly hissing, like the Puff Adder (*Bitis arietans arietans*) – as a form of self-defence if threatened. You will not often encounter snakes on the main footpaths on Table Mountain, but you may come across them –particularly the Puff Adder and/or the Cape Cobra (*Naja nivea*) – in the Cape of Good Hope section of the Park in summer. If you encounter a snake, retreat slowly or give it a wide berth. DO NOT UNDER ANY CIRCUMSTANCES PICK UP A SNAKE, even if it appears dead; some – like the highly venomous Rinkhals (*Hemachatus haemachatus*) – are adept at playing dead. Always wear stout shoes or hiking boots when walking on the mountain. If someone is bitten, try to keep him or her as calm and quiet as possible, and seek medical help immediately. If possible identify the snake, but don't risk another bite. Bind the affected area with a firm pressure bandage and immobilise the limb with a splint. DON'T apply a tourniquet. If the victim finds breathing difficult, apply artificial respiration.
■ Tygerberg Poison Unit:
✆(021)931-6129.

■ INSECTS

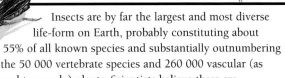

Dinner: A *Hemipepsis* Spider-hunting Wasp with its favourite Rain Spider prey.

Insects are by far the largest and most diverse life-form on Earth, probably constituting about 55% of all known species and substantially outnumbering the 50 000 vertebrate species and 260 000 vascular (as opposed to woody) plants. Scientists believe there are probably more than six million different insect species, although the number described scientifically is fewer than one million. Insects play a crucial ecological role, particularly in pollinating plants. As is the case virtually everywhere else in the world, the number of insects occurring in the fynbos region – and hence in the Park – is not known with any certainty, and new discoveries are being made constantly; for example, one researcher found 12 new species of oil-collecting bees in less than two years in the fynbos region.

However, a great deal of research has been done in recent years, and because of the remarkable richness of fynbos flora, scientists are discovering a correspondingly rich and fascinating insect life, many species of which are endemic: occurring naturally only in this region, and some only in the Park.

Attracted to r
A Ta
Mount.
Beauty visi
Haemant.
or A
F.
flo

SMALL, BEAUTIFUL … AND VERY EFFICIENT

ALTHOUGH MANY FYNBOS PLANTS are pollinated by birds and mammals, the vast majority are pollinated by insects such as beetles, flies, bees, moths and butterflies. Some of these insects are themselves the pollinating agent, while others assist the pollination process by acting as a food source for the agent, such as birds. A single Sugarbush protea flowerhead, for example, can contain literally hundreds of insects of many different species, while other plants are so specialised that the nectar – and pollen – in their flowers can only be accessed by a single species of long-tongued fly. These flies, about the size of large bees, are remarkable in that their rapier-like tongues can be three times as long as their bodies, or nearly five times in the case of one species which occurs on the Cape Flats.

Although there are at least 53 species of butterfly in the Park, this is a small number relative to the huge number of plant species – probably because the tough and nutrient-poor leaves of most fynbos plants do not provide sufficient nutrition for their larvae. One of the most remarkable is the Table Mountain Beauty or Mountain Pride butterfly (*Aeropetes tulbaghia*, formerly *Meneris tulbaghia*), an extremely large, brown butterfly with yellow markings and characteristic blue "eyes" on its wings. It is strongly attracted to the colour red – it will even investigate a red shirt or red hat worn by a hiker. It is the exclusive pollinator of at least 15 plant species – believed to be a world record – which all produce red flowers. These include the Red Crassula (*Crassula coccinea*), many autumn-flowering geophytes (bulbous plants) like the Guernsey Lily (*Nerine sarniensis*), and the Red Disa (*Disa uniflora*), also known as the Pride of Table Mountain. Botanists searched for many years for the pollinator of this beautiful disa before Rudolf Marloth, the "Father of Fynbos", made the dramatic discovery in 1895.

Singular mission: The Table Mountain Beauty, also called the Mountain Pride butterfly, is the pollinator of the Red Disa.

Specialist of the fynbos: The long-tongued fly (*Moegistorhynchus longirostris*) pollinates a wide range of long-tubed white or pink flowers on the wing.

A LINK TO THE PAST

The Velvet Worm, or Peripatus, is one of the remarkable invertebrates of Table Mountain. This animal (not technically an insect) has remained virtually unchanged for some 530 million years. It was long considered an 'evolutionary link' between primitive life forms – the segmented worms, like earthworms – and the more modern arthropods (having a hard, jointed external skeleton), such as insects and millipedes. However, advances in genetics have now allowed scientists to suggest that the Peripatus is itself a specialised arthropod, rather than an ancestor of arthropods. Four *Peripatopsis* species have been recorded in the Park, of which two are endemic to Table Mountain. One, unfortunately, has not been seen for 50 years and may be extinct.

SEED-BEARERS

About 20% of all plants in the Park rely on ants – like the Pugnacious Ant (*Anoplolepis custodiens*) – to disperse their seeds: a strategy called myrmecochory. The ants carry the seeds down into their underground nests where they are safe from predation by small rodents and other seed-eaters, and also from fire. The ants do this for an important food source attached to the seeds: nutrient-rich elaiosomes in the form of a knob or coating. The ants eat the elaiosomes and discard the seeds, many of which remain underground to germinate. The Argentine Ant (*Linepithema humile*), an aggressive alien invasive, has displaced indigenous ants in some areas. This alien ant eats the elaiosomes on the surface and doesn't carry the seeds below ground. Hence it has a very negative effect on fynbos regeneration in places.

Beast to beauty: The Citrus Swallowtail butterfly (*Papilio demodocus*) and its colourful caterpillar.

Statuesque: A Common Green Mantid (*Sphodromantis gastrica*) strikes a classic 'prayer' posture.

Curious creature: The long-snouted Restio Leaf-hopper (*Cephalelus* sp) is perfectly disguised.

CREATURES OF THE DARK

Highly specialised invertebrates, some of them insects, live in the cave system on Table Mountain, and at least 21 are endemic to the Park. These endemics include the Cave Cricket (*Speleiacris tabulae*) that lives mainly on fungus-coated bat droppings and the pure white Cave Peripatus (*Peripatopsis alba*) that preys on the cricket. The blind Cave Shrimp (*Spelaeogriphus lepidops*), above, is the sole survivor in a family that was common millions of years ago, and one of only two living species in an entire order (an order is a scientific grouping higher than a family). The Harvestman (*Speleomontia cavernicola*) is another Park endemic.

WARNING COLOURS

There are at least 3 000 species of beetle in the Park, most dependent on indigenous plants for their survival. Be careful to avoid those of the family Meloidae, the so-called Blister Beetles, which have distinctive bright red or yellow patches on their black abdomens. They exude an extremely toxic substance called cantharadin, which causes blistering of the skin or, if swallowed, haemorrhaging. The beetles' bright colours serve as a warning to would-be predators. One species is called the CMR Beetle, because their black and yellow colours are the same as those of a local regiment, the Cape Mounted Rifles.

Busy: The Cape Honey Bee (*Apis mellifera capensis*) sips nectar from an *Erica baccans* – specially adapted to bee pollination

Amazing metamorphosis: Starting life as an ugly grub the Spotted Veld Antlion (*Palpares speciosus*) turns into a lovely winged adult.

Carpenter Bee
Xylocopa caffra

Damselfly
Sub-order Zygoptera

Table Mountain Beauty
Aeropetes tulbaghia

Cape Honey Bee
Apis mellifera capensis

Mating Heady Maiden
moths
Syntomis cerbera

Citrus Swallowtail
Papilio demodocus

Red-banded Blister Beetle
Actenodia curtula

Fynbos Blue
Tarucus thespis

Mating Garden Acraeas
Acraea horta

Green-headed Blister Beetle
Lytta nitidula

Cape Lappet Moth larva
Pachypasa capensis

Rain Spider
Palystes castaneus

Glittering Monkey Beetles
Anisonyx ditus

African Monarch larva
Danaus chrysippus

Rhinoceros Beetle
Oryctes boas

Common Metallic
Longhorn
Promeces longipes

Green Protea Beetle
Trichostetha fascicularis

Green Grooved
Dung Beetle
Scarabaeus rugosus

Banded-legged
Golden Orb-Web
Spider
Nephila senegalensis

Obese Lily Weevil
Brachycerus obesus

Water Beetles
Dytiscidae
Family

⚠ Boomslang
Dispholidus typus

⚠ Cape Cobra
Naja nivea

⚠ Berg Adder
Bitis atropos

Mole Snake
Pseudapsis cana

Common Egg Eater
Dasypeltis scabra

Western Leopard Toad
Bufo pantherinus

Cape Rain Frog
Breviceps gibbosus

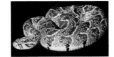

⚠ Puff Adder
(above & below)
Bitis arietans

⚠ Rinkhals
Hemachatus haemachatus

Cape Sand Snake
Psammophis leightoni leightoni

Angulate Tortoise
Chersina angulata

Parrot-beaked Tortoise
Homopus areolatus

Cape River Frog
Afrana fuscigula

Southern Rock Agama
Agama atra

Black Girdled Lizard
Cordylus niger

Cape Dwarf Chameleon
Bradypodion pumilum

Cape Skink
Mabuya capensis

Marsh or Helmeted
Terrapin
Pelomedusa subrufa

Arum Lily Frog
Hyperolius horstocki

■ LAND BIRDS OF THE PARK

Red-winged
Starling

Speckled
Mousebird

Cape Weaver

The fynbos vegetation
which dominates much of
the Park does not support
the large numbers or variety
of birds often found in
other South African
habitats. Those
which do occur
here, however,
include
interesting local
endemic
species and
others which
perform a
vital
ecological
role.

Southern
Double-collared
Sunbird

QUALITY, NOT QUANTITY, FOR FYNBOS BIRDS

THE BIRDS YOU ARE LIKELY TO SEE will vary tremendously according to the composition and age of the vegetation – recently-burnt veld will attract open-country species, whereas old veld with mature shrubs will support very different species. Top of the "most-wanted" list of most birding visitors, and gratifyingly easy to see, are the Cape Sugarbird (*Promerops cafer*) and Orange-breasted Sunbird (*Anthobaphes violacea*), both endemic to fynbos. With its disproportionately long tail – almost 40cm in some males – and distinctive rattling call, the Cape Sugarbird is one of the most familiar birds in mature shrubby fynbos wherever there are proteas, pincushions or Mimetes in flower. The male makes a distinctive *frrt-frrt* sound with its wings in display: specially shaped, bulging flight feathers are used to make this noise. The long, curved bill of the sugarbird is designed to probe the inflorescences for nectar, and pollen which sticks to the feathers on its forehead is transferred to other flowers.

Brimstone Canary (Bully Canary)

The sugarbird also feeds on insects visiting the proteas, especially during the breeding season when extra protein is required.

The Orange-breasted Sunbird also feeds from proteas, but is more intimately linked with the tubular flowers of the 100 or more species of Erica heaths whose corollas match the curve and length of this sunbird's bill. The sunbird is an important pollinator of these plants.

Don't be confused by Red-winged Starlings (*Onychognathus morio*) with bright yellow foreheads in spring! These have been feeding at Tree Pincushion (*Leucospermum conocarpodendron*) flowers. This conspicuous and

I **NEW BIRD NAMES**
All names and binomials are from the Roberts' VII Bird List as at December 2003.

adaptable bird is common throughout the Peninsula, and will certainly greet you at the Cape Point car park. It eats virtually anything and is, unfortunately, a major disperser of the seeds of the invasive Rooikrans (▲ 62/5). Winter and spring are the best times for flowering proteas and heaths and many other birds take advantage of the nectar feast, so any patch of proteas or pincushions in bloom is worth investigating. Watch for the sunbirds and sugarbirds joined by generalist (broad-diet) feeders such as the Cape Weaver (*Ploceus capensis*), Cape White-eye (*Zosterops capensis*), Cape Bulbul (*Pycnonotus capensis*) and others. The specialist nectar-feeders are present all year in fynbos, but are more thinly scattered and less active in summer and autumn.

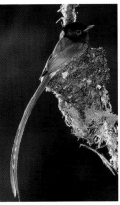

Cape White-eye and chicks

African Paradise-Flycatcher   Cape Batis (male on left)

THE BIRDS FOUND IN STRANDVELD (coastal thicket) are generally quite different to the species found in the fynbos vegetation. Many more insectivorous and generalist species occur here – Southern Boubou (*Laniarius ferrugineus*), Bokmakierie (*Telophorus zeylonus*), Cape Robin-Chat (*Cossypha caffra*), Fiscal Flycatcher (*Sigelus silens*), Karoo Prinia (*Prinia maculosa*) and the like, which are often very scarce in, or completely absent from, fynbos proper.

As in fynbos, the species and numbers of birds in coastal thicket may vary seasonally. More birds occur when berry-bearing shrubs such as Milkwood (*Sideroxylon inerme*), Kraaibessie (*Rhus* spp) and Sea Guarri (*Euclea racemosa*) are fruiting. In spring, the bird-pollinated Bruinsalie (*Salvia*) attracts opportunist Cape Bulbul and Cape White-eye in addition to the nectarivorous Malachite Sunbird (*Nectarinia famosa*) and Southern Double-collared Sunbird (*Cinnyris chalybeus*). In disturbed, sandy areas, Bokdoring (*Lycium*) attracts Speckled Mousebird (*Colius striatus*) and Brimstone Canary (*Serinus sulphuratus*) to its berries as well as the Southern Double-collared Sunbird which drinks nectar from the small flowers and catches the insects which share its predilection for nectar. Overall, the average density of birds in coastal shrub habitats can be 12 times that found in mature proteaceous fynbos

Malachite Sunbird

and 50 times that of recently-burnt restio veld where the odd Plain-backed Pipit (*Anthus leucophrys*), Cape Longclaw (*Macronyx capensis*) and Crowned Lapwing (*Vanellus coronatus*) might be present, if indeed there are any birds at all. One reason is that coastal thickets are less prone to fire than fynbos.– *Mike Fraser*

THE FYNBOS SPECIALS

Although more than 250 land and freshwater bird species occur in fynbos, just six are endemic: Cape Sugarbird (*Promerops cafer*), Cape Rock-jumper (*Chaetops frenatus*), Victorin's Warbler (*Cryptillas victorini*), Cape Siskin (*Pseudo-chloroptila totta*),

▲
Cape Sugarbird

▲
Cape Siskin

Orange-breasted Sunbird (*Anthobaphes violacea*)

▲
Orange-breasted Sunbird

and the Protea Seedeater (*Serinus leucopterus*). Three of these – the rock-jumper, warbler and seedeater – do not occur in the Park although they may all be seen within an hour's drive of Cape Town.

Cape Grassbird

WHERE TO WATCH BIRDS Ⓘ ▲ 84

RAPTORS OF THE PARK

Rock Kestrel

EAGLE
TERRITORY

Perhaps as many as seven or eight pairs of Verreaux's Eagle (Black Eagle) once nested in the Peninsula. In 2004, however, this had been reduced to just one pair resident along the western reaches of Table Mountain, with a second territory occasionally active on the Karbonkelberg, between Hout Bay and Sandy Bay. There is no obvious reason for this decrease in the eagle population, although habitat loss and declines in the abundance of Rock Hyrax (Dassie) – the eagle's favourite prey – may be implicated. Probably the best place to see Verreaux's Eagle is around the Upper Cableway Station, but they are also regularly seen throughout the Park.

MASTERS OF THE SKIES

THE PARK SUPPORTS MANY raptors including eagle, hawk, buzzard, kite, kestrel and falcon. At least 12 species are regular breeding residents, with a further 12 or more occurring as migrants, visitors or vagrants to the area. Five raptor species attain exceptional densities in the Park: Peregrine Falcon (*Falco peregrinus*), Rock Kestrel (*F. rupicolis*), Rufous-chested Sparrowhawk (*Accipiter rufiventris*), African Goshawk (*A. tachiro*) and Black Sparrowhawk (*A. melanoleucus*). Of the resident species, the Jackal Buzzard (*Buteo rufofuscus*) and Forest Buzzard (*B. trizonatus*) are unique to southern Africa.

Jac
Buzz

SKYDIVER – A PARK SPECIAL

Superb hunter: The magnificent Peregrine Falcon can reach a speed of 380 km/h in a stoop. Below, chicks wait for a meal.

NEW BIRD NAMES
All names and binomials are from the Roberts' VII Bird List as at December 2003.

1	Rufous-chested Sparrowhawk
2	Black Sparrowhawk
3	African Marsh-Harrier
4	African Goshawk
5	Forest Buzzard

Verreaux's Eagle: No more than two pairs bred on the Cape Peninsula in early 2004.

Another two – the African Marsh-Harrier (*Circus ranivorus*) and the Peregrine Falcon – are listed as threatened locally.

Along the Peninsula mountain chain, look for the Verreaux's Eagle (*Aquila verreauxii*), an impressive, coal-black bird with striking white markings.

WHERE TO WATCH BIRDS ▲ 84 **I**

The local population of this species is small but they can be seen almost anywhere in the Park. The spectacular Peregrine Falcon is a Park "special". Generally rare in the rest of South Africa, the Peregrine occurs quite commonly and widely on the Peninsula, especially in the more rugged areas with high, sheer rock-faces. The Jackal Buzzard is an attractive, broad-winged, red-chested species, frequently seen in the southern half of the Park, wind-hovering over tracts of open fynbos.

In the forested areas, look out for three common but secretive accipiters (short-winged, long-tailed hawks): Rufous-chested Sparrowhawk, Black Sparrowhawk – both usually found in stands of exotic pines and eucalypts – and African Goshawk, common in thicker stands of exotic poplars or in indigenous bush. In summer, the Forest Buzzard is regularly seen circling over the pine plantations on the eastern slopes of the mountain, between Silvermine and Rhodes Memorial; the European Honey-Buzzard (*Pernis apivorus*) – a rare migrant to South Africa – can sometimes be seen here.

The African Fish-Eagle (*Haliaeetus vocifer*) is an icon of the continent because of its evocative cry and photogenic presence. Many people think it only occurs in places like the Okavango Delta, but in fact it's found in both the central and southern sections of the Park, as is the African Marsh-Harrier. Look for both these birds in the Noordhoek wetlands (▲60). – *Andrew Jenkins*

MARINE BIRDS

Shy Albatross is one of the many seabirds which you can see off the Peninsula's west coast in winter. The birds are rarely as close as this one, however, so binoculars or a telescope are a necessity!

The Park's most famous seabirds are the African Penguins of Boulders (▲ 138/9), but the area is extremely rich in other marine bird species, and the Park is one of the best places in the world to watch truly pelagic bird species from the land.

GREAT VIEWING BUT YOU MAY GET WET

LOOK AFTER OUR OYKS!
Please respect the sanctuary area of Die Mond in the Cape of Good Hope section of the Park as this is one of the last undisturbed stretches of coastline in the Peninsula and an important area for the endangered African Black Oystercatcher (commonly called 'Oyks'). About 100 pairs of this species nest in this section of the Park, as well as a range of other shorebirds.

MANY SPECIES WHICH BREED in the Antarctic or on distant Sub-Antarctic islands, such as Prince Edward, Marion and Tristan da Cunha, spend their winter in the food-rich waters of the Benguela upwelling which washes the Peninsula's west coast. Thousands of birds may be seen, including Atlantic Yellow-nosed, Black-browed and Shy Albatrosses (*Thalassarche chlororhynchos, T. melanophris, T. cauta*), Northern and Southern Giant-Petrels (*Macronectes halli, M. giganteus*), Wilson's Storm-Petrel (*Oceanites oceanicus*), White-chinned Petrel (*Procellaria aequinoctialis*), Sooty Shearwater (*Puffinus griseus*) and Subantarctic Skua (*Catharacta antarctica*). Any headland along the west coast is a potentially good seawatching spot, although shelter is at a premium during the strong westerly winds and often wet conditions which bring the seabirds closest to the shore. An easily accessible spot is Kommetjie. Look out here for roosting cormorant (four species) and Antarctic Tern (*Sterna vittata*) on the rocks. In summer, False Bay is often invaded by huge flocks of Cape Gannet (*Morus capensis*) and Cape Cormorant (*Phalacrocorax capensis*) following shoals of pilchards. These "feeding frenzies", which can draw up to 25 000 Cape Gannet and 250 000 Cape Cormorant at a time, make a spectacular sight. At this time of year, the albatrosses and petrels are replaced by migrant seabirds from the northern hemisphere, such as Sabine's Gull (*Larus sabini*) and Cory's Shearwater (*Calonectris diomedea*). These, and the resident Swift Tern (*Sterna bergii*) and visiting Common and Sandwich Tern (*S. hirundo, S. sandvicensis*) are often harried by Parasitic Jaeger (Arctic Skua) (*Stercorarius parasiticus*), brown, gull-like avian pirates from the north.
The Peninsula's beaches are home to a variety of waders

Petrel collection: Wilson's Storm-Petrel (which will only be seen flying in this region), White-chinned Petrel and Southern Giant-Petrel can be seen offshore in winter.

NEW BIRD NAMES
All names and binomials are from the Roberts' VII Bird List as at December 2003.

(generally long-legged, long-billed shorebirds). The most important resident breeding species is the African Black Oystercatcher (*Haematopus moquini*). This unmistakable bird feeds largely on shellfish, such as limpets, which it prises from the rocks at low tide. It breeds on sandy beaches in midsummer and is very susceptible to disturbance by people and dogs – please take care! The other resident wader likely to be encountered is the White-fronted Plover

Cape Cormorant

(*Charadrius marginatus*). This small, pale bird is most common on the Peninsula's west coast. It nests on sandy beaches and is also vulnerable to disturbance. It takes precautions before leaving the nest, by scuffing sand over its eggs to make them less conspicuous.

In summer the Cape beaches are home to thousands of migrant waders from the tundra of northern Russia and Fennoscandinavia. The most abundant are Sanderling (*Calidris alba*), Curlew Sandpiper (*C. ferruginea*) and Ruddy Turnstone (*Arenaria interpres*). Smaller numbers of Common Greenshank (*Tringa nebularia*); Common Whimbrel (*Numenius phaeopus*); Red Knot (*Calidris canutus*); Common Ringed and Grey Plover (*Charadrius hiaticula, Pluvialis squatarola*) are also found along the coast. The west coast of the Peninsula is best

Visitor from the north: Arctic Tern (*Sterna paradisaea*).

for waders, where the mounds of stranded and decaying seaweed provide rich foraging for Beach Hoppers (*Talorchestia capensis*) and other invertebrate food. The False Bay coastline is much less productive and there is too much human disturbance. Cormorants can be seen along the entire coastline, either roosting on the rocks or feeding offshore. White-breasted (*Phalacrocorax lucidus*) and Cape Cormorant breed on the cliffs at Cape Point. Kelp and Hartlaub's Gull (*Larus dominicanus, L. hartlaubii*) will join you in any coastal car park on the chance of some picnic scraps. With all shorebirds, please keep disturbance to a minimum or avoid approaching them at all; they can be best observed from a distance through binoculars. They need all the time they can get to feed, preen and rest on the beaches undisturbed. A bit like us, really. – *Mike Fraser*

Kelp Gull: A coastal resident.

The gathering: Terns and gulls at Kommetjie.

WHERE TO WATCH BIRDS ▲ 84

Common sight: The White-breasted Cormorant is the largest cormorant in the region.

Atlantic Yellow-nosed Albatross

WATCHING THE MIGRANTS
Spring and autumn, when migrant seabirds are on the move and summer and winter visitors overlap for a few weeks, can provide the Park birder with an almost unmatched richness of pelagic species. The best sea-watching site is the rock ledges above the Cape of Good Hope car park (pictured below), but this is a very exposed and potentially dangerous area, so do take care.

Cape Sugarbird

Below: Pied Avocets (*Recurvirostra avosetta*) on the beach at Olifantsbos

Red-chested Cuckoo (juv)

Helmeted Guineafowl

Cape Siskin

Cape Gannet

I GETTING CONNECTED
For more on birds in the Park, contact the Buffelsfontein Visitor Centre, ✆ (021) 780-9204, or Cape Birding Route, ✆ (021) 785-7680
Websites: **www. birding-africa.com or www. capebirdingroute .org**

TWITCHING IN SPLENDID SURROUNDINGS

THE VARIETY OF HABITATS within a relatively small area makes the Park an exciting location for birders. These habitats, each with their own particular birds, extend from rocky mountain tops through fynbos scrub, forested ravines and down to coastal wetlands, beaches and the open sea. Although not supporting the species richness and abundance of birds found in some other parts of South Africa, there is still plenty to see, including some range-restricted specialities and spectacular concentrations of waterbirds and seabirds. Some of the best birding sites are also popular visitor destinations, so you can enjoy famous landmarks and landscapes while looking for birds.

Table Mountain is a must for visitors but is not the most brilliant place for birds. The sparse vegetation on the summit plateau does, however, support Orange-breasted Sunbird (*Anthobaphes violacea*), Ground Woodpecker (*Geocolaptes olivaceus*), Cape Rock-Thrush (*Monticola rupestris*), Neddicky (*Cisticola fulvicapilla*) and Cape Grassbird (*Sphenoeacus afer*), among others, with African Black Swift (*Apus barbatus*) and Alpine Swift (*Tachymarptis melba*) overhead. All these can also be seen on the adjoining Lion's Head. Look out for White-necked Raven (*Corvus albicollis*) here as well. Kirstenbosch National Botanic Garden is probably your best bet for the Cape Sugarbird (*Promerops cafer*). Birdwatching here couldn't be easier and you will be probably be accompanied by Cape Spurfowl (*Ptemistis capensis*) trotting over the lawns and African Black Swift hawking above you. The forested slopes above Kirstenbosch are good for African Olive-Pigeon (*Columba arquatrix*), Cape Batis (*Batis capensis*) and, in summer, African Paradise-Flycatcher (*Terpsiphone viridis*) and Red-chested Cuckoo (*Cuculus solitarius*) (Piet-my-vrou). The site's most sought-after bird, the rare and secretive Knysna Warbler (*Bradypterus sylvaticus*), may require some inside information and an early start as it's best located singing at dawn at a few densely-vegetated sites.

Fynbos birding is also relatively good in the Silvermine and Cape of Good Hope sections of the Park, although the

African Wood-Ow[l]

Southern Double-collared Sunbird

Southern Boubou

Bokmakierie

Fiscal Flycatcher

BIRDING BEYOND THE PARK

Karoo Prinia

A good birding site on the Peninsula outside the Park is Rondevlei Nature Reserve (▲158), which is a great spot for waterbirds and a variety of bush birds. The nearby Strandfontein Sewage Works is internationally famous for its waterbirds, including flamingos, numerous egrets, herons, ducks, waders and terns, all easily viewed from the comfort of your car. Beyond the Peninsula, but within easy reach of Cape Town, the West Coast National Park (▲160) and nearby estuarine and saltpan habitats are superb for waders and other waterbirds. To the east, the De Hoop area near Cape Agulhas (▲162) combines fynbos, thicket, freshwater and seabirds in a superb landscape and has tremendous birding opportunities.

Cape Spurfowl

number of birds you encounter can be quite low, which is a fairly typical scenario in this habitat. Try to find a patch of flowering proteas or ericas to be sure of sunbirds and other nectar feeders. The Cape Point viewing sites are a reliable spot for Cape Siskin (*Pseudochloroptila totta*), a fynbos endemic. Cape Rock-Thrush (*Monticola rupestris*) and Ground Woodpecker (*Geocolaptes olivaceus*) also appear occasionally here. When visiting the African Penguins at Boulders (▲138), don't ignore the coastal thicket as it supports a good variety of species including White-backed and Speckled Mousebirds (*Colius colius, C. striatus*), Southern Boubou (*Laniarius ferrugineus*), Bokmakierie (*Telophorus zeylonus*), Brimstone Canary (*Serinus sulphuratus*) and Cape Canary (*S. canicollis*), Karoo Prinia (*Prinia maculosa*) and Southern Double-collared Sunbird (*Cinnyris chalybeus*). There is also good thicket vegetation at Olifantsbos. When in flower, the *Leonotis* (Wild Dagga) patch here is excellent for Malachite Sunbird (*Nectarinia famosa*) and Southern Double-collared Sunbird.

In summer, Olifantsbos Bay supports good numbers of waders such as Curlew Sandpiper (*Calidris ferruginea*) Pied Avocet (*Recurvirostra avosetta*) and Ruddy Turnstone (*Arenaria interpres*). These are often joined by such unlikely "shorebirds" as African Sacred Ibis (*Threskiornis aethiopicus*), Helmeted Guineafowl (*Numida meleagris*), Plain-backed Pipit (*Anthus leucophrys*) and Southern Red Bishop (*Euplectes orix*) which feed on kelp-fly larvae and sandhoppers amongst the decaying seaweed. Any stretch of coast between Noordhoek and Bordjiesrif/Buffels Bay is worth checking for waders and other intertidal species. Kommetjie, the Cape of Good Hope and Cape Point are well placed for watching pelagic seabirds. Glencairn (not in the Park) can be outstanding for large numbers of shearwaters, skuas, terns and Sabine's Gull (*Larus sabini*) in spring and autumn during a strong south-easter. –
Mike Fraser

■ MARINE LIFE IN THE PARK

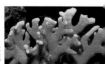

Bold colours:
Noble Coral

The seas off southern Africa are dominated by two major oceanographic systems: the powerful Agulhas Current, which sweeps down the east coast at up to five knots (2.6m per second), bringing warm water from the tropics (the Indian Ocean); and the cold Benguela current which drifts northwards off the west coast, fed by the upwelling of icy but nutrient-rich water. The Cape Peninsula is a transitional zone between these two systems, giving it an incredibly rich and varied marine flora and fauna as a result.

CURRENTS OF LIFE

ON THE EAST COAST, the core of the Agulhas Current flows along the edge of the continental shelf: that point at which the relatively shallow coastal waters suddenly get much deeper, occurring roughly at about the 100 fathom, or 200m, mark. From about central Transkei, the continental shelf moves away from the coast and the Agulhas Current follows, swinging southwards and sending off several huge anti-clockwise gyres as it flows before eventually swinging back on its tracks to become the east-flowing Return Agulhas Current. This phenomenon, known as retroflection, can occur anywhere between Cape Agulhas and a position

Precious resource: The West Coast Rock Lobster.

well to the west of Cape Point, in the Atlantic Ocean. This is why the Loggerhead Turtle (*Caretta caretta*) and the Leatherback Turtle (*Dermochelys coriacea*) which use this current to move from the breeding ground of Zululand, are occasionally seen from the shores of the Park.

On the west coast, cold water drifts northwards on the Benguela Current towards the shallower coastal area. Here, in summer, the seasonal southerly and south-easterly winds that blow offshore push the surface water which

WHERE THE OCEANS MEET

Is it possible to plot a line somewhere off the southern tip of Africa that marks the exact meeting point of the Indian Ocean and the Atlantic Ocean? Yes – but only if you're a map-maker more concerned with cartographic symmetry than with physical reality. In that case, you'd simply draw a line south from Cape Agulhas and write Atlantic on the left and Indian on the right. But in fact these two oceans don't meet so much as merge, and this merging is an intangible, constantly shifting phenomenon that occurs anywhere over a distance of 100 nautical miles or more, depending on weather, season and various oceanographic factors. However, if you choose marine communities as the criterion to distinguish between the two oceans, then Cape Point is definitely the dividing line, because there are marked differences between the species that occur in the seas on either side of this famous landmark.

Atlantic Ocean

upwelling

Benguela Current

Biogeographic divide: Cape Point

Most southerly point: Cape Agulhas

retroflection

Agulhas Current

Indian Ocean

Return Agulhas Current

Graceful: The shy but intelligent Common Octopus.

Shore Crab

has been warmed by the sun more or less parallel to the coast, but Coriolis forces (forces caused by the rotation of the Earth) deflect it westwards, out to sea. The resulting water "vacuum" just off the coast is then filled with the very cold water rising from the depths and bringing with it rich nutrients that have accumulated in this dark zone; this phenomenon is known as upwelling. Both of these systems have a profound effect on the region's marine biotic communities.

A RICH AND FASCINATING DIVERSITY

MARINE BIOLOGISTS DEFINE FIVE "biogeographic provinces" along the southern African coastline which are the collective habitat of more than 10 000 species of marine plants and animals – almost 15% of the world total of coastal marine species. Two of these provinces shape the marine life of the Park: the cool temperate Namaqua Province on the west coast between Luderitz (Namibia) and Cape Point, and the warm temperate Agulhas Province on the south and east coasts between Cape Point and northern Transkei. The differences between these provinces are extreme, and explain the rich and varied marine life around the Park's shores. Because of upwelling, the west coast is very productive and there are rich food chains, starting with microscopic floating plants called phytoplankton

which thrive on the upwelled nutrients. The food chains culminate in equally rich fisheries: hake, pilchards and anchovy, among others. The western coast is characterised by dense and prolific kelp beds, particularly Sea Bamboo (*Ecklonia maxima*) and Split-fan Kelp (*Laminaria pallida*). These kelp beds provide food and shelter (they break the force of the waves) for many animals and plants, including abalone (perlemoen), rock lobster, sea urchins, mussels, sea cucumbers and algal plants. But despite its extremely high productivity, there are relatively few marine species on the west coast compared to the warmer east coast. The greater diversity of the east coast is mainly because of its large array of tropical Indo-Pacific species, many of

Prolific: Split-fan Kelp

which extend as far west as False Bay, including a number of crabs and coral species which cannot tolerate cooler water. As well as biogeographic provinces, scientists also define five major marine habitats: rocky intertidal shores, sandy beaches, kelp beds, estuaries and the open ocean. All of these occur in or around the Park, but the few estuaries within its boundaries are very small and relatively insignificant. Marine animals and plants which Park visitors can expect to see include the beautiful but shy octopus; limpets (particularly *Scutellastra cochlear* – previously *Patella cochlear* – which can reach amazing densities of up to 2 600 per square metre!); red-bait; barnacles; scores of species of red, brown and green algae (seaweeds); whelks; plough snails; sea urchins; sea anemones; starfish; white and black mussels; beach hoppers – kelp-eating amphipods; rockpool fish like gobies, blennies and klipfishes (literally "rock" fish); and hermit crabs (not true crabs), among many others. In this limited space it's impossible to give more than the very briefest outline; Park visitors should consult the excellent books available (▲ 181).

1
2	3	4
5	7
6
8

1. Goose barnacles
2. Perlemoen
3. Sea urchins
4. Feather star
5. Alikreukel
6. Puffer fish
7. Sea fan
8. Basket star

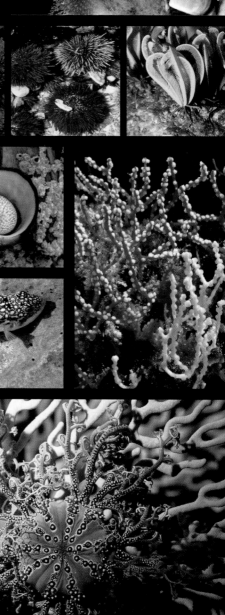

1. Anemone
2. Soft coral
3. Pink hermit crab
4. Paper nautilus
5. Palmate sea fan
6. Dark shyshark
7. Southern Right Whale

Originally, right whales were named for precisely that reason: they were the "right" whales to catch because they were slow; produced large amounts of blubber (fat), meat and baleen (whale bone); and floated once they had been harpooned, making recovery easy. Now, happily, right whales are aptly named for another reason: they are the "right" whales to watch because they come very close inshore during their annual winter migration to the Cape coast and are easily viewed and photographed.

MAKING A BIG SPLASH

OTHER WHALES IN OUR WATERS

Two other whale species are also seen from the Park: the Humpback Whale (*Megaptera novaeangliae*) and Bryde's Whale (*Balaenoptera edeni*). The Humpback is a very energetic species, renowned for its spectacular breaching which can involve leaping right out of the water. Humpbacks are easily distinguished from right whales by their single blow, arched back with a fin in the middle, and long, narrow flippers. The Bryde's Whale has a single blow and a small fin set near the end of its back, but does not often expose itself. The giant Blue Whale (*Balaenoptera musculus*), the largest living creature, has very occasionally been sighted in Cape waters in recent times, but not from the Park's coastline.

ALTHOUGH WALKER BAY PRIDES ITSELF on being the Cape's whale-watching centre, there are many good vantage points in the Park to see whales.

The whale most frequently seen from the Park is the Southern Right Whale (*Eubalaena australis*). Right whales are baleen whales, meaning they have large plates of baleen – made from keratin, similar to human fingernails – hanging from their upper jaws. The hairy inner edge of these baleen plates is used to sieve prey from the water: these are copepods, a tiny form of plankton only a few millimetres long which occur in dense swarms.

Adult female right whales average about 14m in length and weigh anywhere between 29 and 58 tonnes (average 41 tonnes), and the males are a bit smaller. Calves, born after a pregnancy of a year or slightly longer, are on average six metres in length, and will probably live for about 50 years. Right whales normally swim at between a half and four kilometres an hour, but can reach 17 km/h during a "sprint".

This species, generally black but some with white on the belly, is characterised by callosities: these are pale brownish, wart-like patches of raised, roughened skin scattered over the head. The colour of the callosities is caused by thousands of tiny crustaceans called amphipods which live on the whale and feed on the dead outer layers of its skin. Each right whale has a distinct pattern of callosities, making it individually recognisable. So by photographing the whales during an annual census, biologists have compiled a highly accurate database of their movements and behaviour. Right whales start migrating back from their summer feeding grounds deep in the Southern Ocean in late April, heading rapidly for warmer coastal waters during May. Peak abundance off the Cape coast is from mid-August to mid-October, and then numbers tail off rapidly, with the last animals usually leaving in January. A very small number do spend the entire season locally.

Below: A Southern Right whale breaches in Peninsula waters.

Slaughter house: The whaling station at Buffels Bay near Cape Point in the early 1900s.

A very long way from home: An occasional visitor is the huge Southern Elephant Seal (*Mirounga leonina*), which sometimes hauls out on local shores during a moult – a long way from its habitat on sub-Antarctic islands like Prince Edward and Marion.

Dolphins are regularly seen from many vantage points in the Park. At least 10 dolphin species have been recorded in Cape waters, but visitors will probably only see the Common Dolphin (*Delphinus delphis*), Dusky Dolphin (*Lagenorhynchus obscurus*) or Bottlenosed Dolphin (*Tursiops truncatus*). The Common Dolphin is often seen in False Bay and off Cape Point, and can hunt in schools of up to 5 000 animals during 'feeding frenzies'. Both Common and Dusky dolphins regularly indulge in the most graceful and dramatic of water ballets. Killer Whales (*Orcinus orca*) are occasionally seen.

I HOT SPOTS TO WATCH WHALES

The cliff viewpoint above Rooikrans in the Cape of Good Hope (Cape Point) section of the Park is an excellent place to watch whales because it overlooks deep water. To get there, drive just over 10km from the main entrance gate and turn left at the traffic circle. This leads to the Rooikrans parking area, and the viewing site is immediately ahead. *Take care here in high winds!* Another particularly rewarding site is along Boyes Drive between Kalk Bay and Muizenberg. Other good viewing spots are the coastal road between Boulders and Smitswinkel Bay, and between Scarborough and Kommetjie (and especially overlooking Slangkop lighthouse). Also try Chapman's Peak Drive, and the road between Llandudno and Bakoven.

BACK FROM THE BRINK

Southern Right Whales are one of the world's great conservation success stories. They were hunted so ferociously that from just 1785 to 1805 an estimated 12 000 were killed along the southern African coast between Walvis Bay and

Delagoa Bay (now Maputo). Although the population collapsed as a result – hardly surprisingly! – shore-based whaling continued through into the 20th century. This species was finally protected in South African waters in 1940, by which stage it was estimated that the population visiting these shores included just 50 or so breeding females. Since then, these right whales have staged a remarkable recovery, and since the 1970s the population has been growing at 7% a year – biologically, the maximum possible for this species whose females give birth to a calf on average once every three years. Today, the total local population is about 3 700 animals and is doubling every 10 years.

■ Hikers on Table Mountain's Back Table, near the dams (▲116/7

■ Penguins watch kayakers off Boulders Beach (▲138/9).

■ A paraglider soars along the Twelve Apostles (▲150/1).

OUT AND ABOUT IN THE PARK

'TAKE NOTHING
BUT
PHOTOGRAPHS,
LEAVE NOTHING
BUT
FOOTPRINTS'

A CODE FOR VISITORS

■ A cyclist enjoys the
view at Cape Point.
(▲ 148/9)

Easy ride: The cableway offers visitors a quick route up Table Mountain.

There's very seldom cause to celebrate the outbreak of war, but Capetonians have at least one reason to be grateful for the start of World War 1 in August 1914 – it stopped in its tracks, literally, the first project for a mechanical device to take people to the summit of Table Mountain. This was a plan for a funicular railway, hauled by a wire rope from

A Verreaux's Eagle (Black Eagle) soars above the mountain

Vista: A telescope from an earlier era.

an engine on the summit, running up Platteklip Gorge. The plan required substantial cuttings which would undoubtedly have severely defaced the front profile of the already world-famous mountain.

▐ SLOW ROUTE TO SUCCESS

Although a novelty when it opened in 1929, the cableway was not an immediate financial success, and two of the financial backers – Sir Ernest Oppenheimer and Sir David Graaff – pulled out of the venture in the depression years of the 1930s. But after World War 2, an ever-increasing number of visitors ensured the project's viability, with the one millionth passenger being recorded in 1959. The second million took only another 11 years and the third million five years after that. At the turn of the century, the total number of passengers stood at 13.3 million.

Top spot: The Upper Cableway Station on the Western Table.

EARLY PLANS TO GET TO THE SUMMIT

I The cableway is totally weather-dependent – and particularly wind-dependent – and therefore does not accept bookings, although there is a voucher system for tour operators. **Always check it's operating before your visit,** © **(021) 424-8181.** The cost is adjusted regularly, but in January 2004 it was R105 return for adults, R55 return for children under 18, R77 return for students with a valid student card, and R55 return for pensioners over 60 with a valid South African identity document. A single fare is close to half. There are regular price 'specials' which are advertised in the media. From 1 December to 31 January, the first car up leaves at 8am, the last car up is at 9pm and the last down at 10pm. In high summer season over Christmas and New Year, opening times are extended. From 1 February to 30 April, the first car up is at 8.30am, the last at 7.30pm and the last car down is at 8.30pm. From May to 30 November, the first car is at 8.30am, the last car up is at 5pm and the last car down is at 6pm. A loud siren at the upper station warns when the last car down is due, or when the cableway is to close because of deteriorating weather.

THE FUNICULAR WAS THE FAVOURED PLAN of two proposals made by Swiss engineer HM Peter of Zurich, who had been invited by the Cape Town City Council in 1912 to devise an easy way to take people to the mountain summit. His other option was for a rack railway – a system in which a locomotive running on cog wheels draws itself up by feeding the cogs into slots on the line – from Kloof Nek, across the corner of Fountain Ravine and onto the Central Table, which would have been an environmental and aesthetic disaster.

Peter estimated the cost of his proposed funicular at £75 000 – a substantial sum in those days. Because of

Limited: The 1974 cars could carry only 28 passengers.

the cost and the controversial nature of the plan, the City Council put the proposal to its ratepayers in the first plebiscite in the city's history in August 1913. The citizens responded positively by 2 939 votes to 1 214, and preliminary work had already started before the outbreak of World War 1 brought the project to an immediate halt.

Because of the post-war depression, nothing further happened until early 1926 when a Norwegian engineer who had emigrated to Cape Town, Trygve Stromsoe, wrote to the Cape Times newspaper proposing a new idea: a cableway – more correctly, a ropeway – carrying cable cars which would offer passengers magnificent views over the city while being safe and reasonably cheap. His proposal caught the eye of influential city businessman Sir Alfred Hennessy, who quickly persuaded other major investors in the form of Sir David Graaff and Sir Ernest Oppenheimer to join him and Stromsoe in forming a company, the Table Mountain Aerial Cableway Company, with a founding capital investment of £10 000.

I A FINE RECORD

The Table Mountain cableway has an enviable safety record. In more than 70 years of operation, there has not been a single fatality resulting from any mechanical failure of either the cable cars or the ropes.

Just opened: An early visitor admires the cableway.

A MOUNTAIN OF A TASK

MAJOR WORK HAD TO DONE before the actual cableway could be constructed, including the building of an access road to the site of the lower cableway station (the first part of the present Tafelberg Road); the erection of a temporary cableway to carry building material to the upper cableway station; and a pump station at the top of Fountain Ravine to supply water to the upper station and restaurant.

Work started on the lower station in December 1927 and on the upper station in June 1928. The buildings, designed by Cape Town architects Walgate and Elsworth, were not to everyone's liking, and some Capetonians complained bitterly about the "pimple" which appeared on the upper profile of their beloved mountain. But the work continued, with the construction team riding up and down in a temporary, open box-car nicknamed "the soapbox". The first full-sized car made the eight-minute journey up on the 1 213m rope span on 9 August 1929, carrying Sir Alfred and Lady Hennessy and Stromsoe, among others. The official opening was performed by the Mayor of Cape Town, the Reverend AJS Lewis, on 4 October 1929.

The main rope, or cable, was renewed in 1958 and again

Hardy: Restios (reeds) thrive on the exposed summit.

Gracing the top: One of many Erica species on Table Mountain.

I **ALL THE INFO**
On the web: **www.tablemountain.net**
For visitor information about the cableway and to check whether it is operating,
℗ (021) 424-8181
To contact the administration of the Table Mountain Aerial Cableway Company,
℗ (021) 424-0015

Careful landscaping: The Upper Cableway Station was redeveloped in 1997.

in 1974, while the plant was renewed in 1967. The original cable cars, which carried 20 passengers and an attendant, were replaced in 1958 with slightly bigger cars carrying 24 passengers each. These were used until 1974, when new, lighter cars were introduced with a passenger load of 28. Then in 1997, the cableway was closed for nine months for a major upgrade and re-design costing R104 million. It re-opened on 4 October 1997 – to the hour and day of the original opening 68 years previously. Refurbishment included new ropes (cables) each weighing 18 tonnes and new aerodynamic cars that carry a maximum of 64 passengers and rotate through 360 degrees during

Rare: Snow does fall on Table Mountain, but rarely ... and it doesn't last long.

the ride to the summit. The cableway is run at a speed of between six and 10 metres per second, depending on how busy it is, so the ride takes anywhere between just over three minutes and nine minutes. The present operation works on a counterweight system weighing 134 tonnes.

USER-FRIENDLY
While the bigger cars and new booking system have not completely eliminated queues during high tourist season, the longest wait now is less than an hour – a far cry from the '70s and '80s when people sometimes waited six hours or longer, often in the full glare of the harsh summer sun, to experience the thrill of a ride on one of the world's premier tourist attractions.

1947: General Smuts escorts the Royal Party on the summit.

Always around:
A Dassie at the Upper Cableway Station. (▲ 66)

ONCE IN A LIFETIME

General Jan Smuts was a traditionalist mountaineer who despised the cableway and he reportedly deigned to use it only once. This was during the Royal Visit of February 1947 when, for reasons of both protocol and political necessity – he was due in Parliament and could not afford the time to walk down – he accompanied the Royal Party down in the cableway. (▲18)

■ SAFE HIKING IN THE PARK

There are some 800km of footpaths in the Park, and while certain popular routes – like Platteklip Gorge or the Bridle Path in Cecilia Forest – can get quite busy on weekends and in high summer, there are more than enough paths and trails to cater for all visitors' needs. If you want to get away from the madding crowd, you can find a quiet spot to yourself. When the weather is fine – or even when it's not but when you're properly

WATER WISDOM
The Giardia parasite, which can cause stomach problems, does occur in Cape Peninsula streams. Many people drink from them but it is best to always take your own water.

equipped for the elements – there are few experiences to beat walking a path on Table Mountain or elsewhere in the Park. But to make the most of this, please adhere to common-sense safety rules. The mountain can, and does, change mood astonishingly quickly and it can be treacherous; every year, unwary, under-prepared or inexperienced walkers or hikers get caught out and suffer as a result. Sadly, they sometimes pay the ultimate price. Be safe, and make the most of the Park's wonderful opportunities.

THE TEN COMMANDMENTS OF HIKING SAFETY

- Don't walk or hike alone; four is the ideal number.
- Choose your route carefully according to ability and experience.
- Every party should have a leader. Walk at the pace of the slowest member, and don't split up.
- Always tell someone where you're going, your intended route and what time you're expected back. Stick to that route.
- If you lose your way, try to retrace your steps – don't push on regardless into a strange area. If possible, stick to broad open slopes; remember that climbing down is more difficult and often more dangerous than climbing up.
- Always take sufficient wind- and waterproof clothing with you, even in mid-summer, and wear sensible walking shoes or hiking boots. Wear a hat or cap in summer and use sunblock. Carry your extras in a rucksack to leave your hands free.
- If lost or forced to stop because of bad weather or some other reason, stay together and remain in one place. Find the closest shelter from wind and rain.
- In case of injury, take time to assess the situation first – the injured person may recover sufficiently to be able to continue. If not, send two people for help and let the third remain with the injured person. If possible, mark the position of the injured person on a map and send it with those going for help.

RESCUE

Mountain Rescue:
✆ (021) 948-9900.
Metro emergency:
✆ 10177, or
Police Flying Squad:
✆ 10111.
In case of difficulty with an emergency call,
✆ 1022.

Safety first: The Park offers wonderful outings, but hikers must be safety conscious.

⚠ **Warning to hikers and climbers:** Wind and cloud can come up very suddenly, causing dangerous conditions and forcing the cableway to close at short notice. Check conditions before setting out if planning to use the cableway to come down.

- Until you know your way around, stick to authorised, well-used paths which will be indicated on the Park-endorsed hiking map and heed the warnings on this map. Don't take shortcuts and especially don't wander into ravines like First and Second Waterfall on Devil's Peak; Window Gorge next to Skeleton above Kirstenbosch; or Slangolie, Fountain or Blinkwater ravines on the Twelve Apostles.

Beautiful but dangerous: India Venster is one of the more popular routes up Table Mountain – but it is not easy and is not recommended for novices.

- Always take sufficient water, especially in summer, and also food in case of a delay. Watch the weather and time, and turn back before you start running late or if bad weather threatens.

Now, you can add an 11th commandment:

- Take a fully-charged cellphone, although it should be switched off as a courtesy to other Park users. There is not cellphone reception throughout the Park, but you will always be able to reach a place where you can use a cellphone more quickly than you'll get to a landline.

DON'T TRY THIS IN YOUR SALAD!

Also known as Mountain celery because of its likeness to the edible plant, the Blister Bush (*Peucedanum galbanum*) has ruined many an outing on the mountain. It is actually a member of the carrot family. Don't touch this plant because you will almost certainly erupt in painful blisters, caused by a compound released during the chemical reaction between strong sunlight and the bruised leaves – a mechanism to deter herbivores. If you've brushed heavily against this plant, cover the affected area immediately to exclude any sunlight. Seek medical advice for any blistering.

■ GENERAL SAFETY AND DOG WALKING

Cape Town is like any other big city in the world. Make the effort to read up about your destination before setting out; exercise the same common-sense, day-to-day safety precautions that you would anywhere else; and don't venture alone into strange places or situations where you feel vulnerable or uncomfortable. Follow this simple advice and the odds are that you will be perfectly safe and have an enjoyable outing.

SETTING OUT WITH CONFIDENCE

THE SAME ADVICE APPLIES TO THE PARK: make sure you know where you're going and what to expect there, and be properly prepared – for example, shorts and a tee-shirt, sandals and a sun hat may be sufficient for a short outing to the beach, but they will definitely not be adequate for a walk up the mountain, even on the hottest day in summer.

■ Read and memorise the "10 Commandments" of mountain safety (▲ 98/9) and the advice on how to handle baboons (▲68/9).

■ Carry a fully-charged cellphone, and make sure you know where to find emergency telephone numbers in a hurry (▲180).

■ Don't litter; carry everything you bring into the Park out again, and take the trouble to pick up other bits of litter those less careful than yourself may have left lying around.

■ Obey the old mountaineering adage: *Take nothing but photographs, leave nothing footprints.* Don't pick, break or trample any plants or flowers, or remove seeds, rocks or plants.

■ Don't deface anything in the Park with graffiti. If you see others doing this, please ask them to stop and report any incidents to the Park officials.

■ Don't attempt to feed, touch or harm any of the animals or birds in the Park – dassies (Rock Hyrax), baboons and the African Penguin all have fierce bites!

■ Never light fires anywhere other than in designated braai (barbecue) areas, and don't ever discard cigarette butts or throw them from car windows, even if they are dead.

The Park is a sensitive area; please treat it with respect and help Park staff conserve this globally unique and much-loved environment.

Here are some general safety tips provided by the SA Police Service:

■ Do not attract unwanted attention by openly displaying cash, expensive jewellery, cameras or other valuables;

■ Avoid carrying large sums of money, particularly foreign currency, on your person;

■ Avoid strange, dark, poorly illuminated or isolated places;

■ In an emergency, don't panic and try to think laterally; try to talk your way out of threatening situations;

■ In a robbery or hijack situation, do as you are told. Do not argue with or challenge your accoster and do not look directly into his eyes. Keep your hands still and visible; if you have to undo a seat belt, ask first.

REMEMBER: You can replace all your valuables and belongings, but never your life.

THE QUESTION OF CAR GUARDS

The Park is an 'open access' system where visitors have an almost limitless number of places where they can park their vehicles and enter on foot. Because the Park has limited financial and manpower resources, providing formal security at all the possible entry points has never been an option for management. Parking areas at many popular entry points – such as Signal Hill – have been targeted by criminals. As is the case elsewhere in the city, small-time entrepreneurs have used this opportunity to provide their services as unofficial car guards in these parking areas. Please note: NONE of these guards is formally employed by the Park, and the Park takes no responsibility for their behaviour or effectiveness. However, most of these car guards are reliable and do provide a valuable service, and it is customary to reward them appropriately. In 2004 prices, R5 for up to half a day or R10 for a full day is considered reasonable. However, you are not obliged to pay, and do not allow yourself to be intimidated into paying if you don't want to. If you are threatened at all, immediately call the police. ✆ 10111, or the Park's 24-hour emergency number, ✆ (021) 957-4700.

■ **Note:** The parking at Silvermine south (Muizenberg side) is now an official pay area.

BEST FRIENDS – WHEN CONTROLLED

THE PARK IS UNIQUE among South Africa's network of 20 national parks because most of it is accessible free to users and, particularly, because these users are allowed to take their dogs with them into most areas. This is because of commitments made when the Park was established in 1998. However, the presence of dogs is contentious, partly because uncontrolled dogs can, and do, have an adverse impact on the Park's ecology, and partly because many visitors do not like dogs and their experience is spoiled by unruly animals.

To resolve these problems, the Park authorities undertook a comprehensive public participation programme around the dog walking issue. This included discussions with an informally constituted group, Friends of the Dog Walkers, which acknowledged that dog ownership conferred special responsibilities in ecologically sensitive areas. A Code of Conduct for dog walking (see at right) and an Environmental Management Programme for walkers accompanied by dogs in the park, were compiled. These can be downloaded from the Park's Website: **www.cpnp.co.za**.

⊖ NO-GO AREAS FOR DOGS

Dogs are not permitted anywhere in:
● The fenced area of the Cape of Good Hope section;
● Orange Kloof above Hout Bay;
● Rhodes Estate game camps on Devil's Peak;
● Klawer Valley restricted military area above Simon's Town;
● Boulders, below Willis Walk; and
● The formal garden area at Kirstenbosch (as determined by the National Botanical Institute).

FOR MORE INFORMATION
Contact the Friends of the Dog Walkers: e-mail **allweath@iafrica.com** or **library@elru.co.za**, or
✆ (021) 671-7451 or ✆ (021) 671-9689

LION'S HEAD WALK ①

①

Popular outing:
Dwarfed by Table Mountain displaying its famous tablecloth, hikers set off among Silver Trees up the path to Lion's Head.

Basking:
Hikers are bound to see rock agamas in warm weather.

WARNING

It has become something of a Cape Town tradition to hike to the summit of Lion's Head and toast the full moon with champagne as it rises over the distant Hottentots Holland mountains to the east. On these festive occasions, the summit can be as packed as a busy Waterfront shopping mall. If you decide to join in the fun, please remember that alcohol, darkness and the initial steep descent can be a very dangerous combination, and there have been several accidents on such occasions, at least one of them fatal.

The view from the 669m summit of Lion's Head is, arguably, the best Cape Town has to offer: a breathtaking 360-degree sweep taking in the city bowl; Devil's Peak and the famous front face of Table Mountain; the majestic Twelve Apostles; the stunning scenery of the Atlantic seaboard from Oudekraal through Bakoven, Camps Bay and Clifton to Sea Point and Green Point; Table Bay and, of course, Robben Island.

Pincu

A NEW VISTA AT EVERY TURN

WHETHER YOU AGREE with this assessment or have your own preference for the Peninsula's top viewing spot, the short and relatively easy walk to the top of Lion's Head is a must for those wanting to savour the very best that the Park has to offer.

To get there, drive up Kloof Nek Road from the city to the circle at the top where you turn hard right up Signal Hill Drive. Drive up about 500m, to a small parking area under a line of tall gum trees on the right.

The route to the top starts with a fairly steep slog up a gravel jeep track which begins opposite the parking area. This is one of the most used routes on the mountain, and the track is initially quite worn and stony. Its condition improves as you climb, though, and stands of lovely Silver Trees (*Leucadendron argenteum*) on either side will help take your mind off the steep incline. This is one of only three areas on Table Mountain where these beautiful trees grow naturally. After about 700m, the jeep track ends in a level open area offering a wonderful view south over Camps Bay towards Oudekraal. Here you will also see one of the two launch ramps used by paragliders on Lion's Head. A wide, easily visible path continues upwards. As you spiral up around the peak, the view changes constantly, and you

At the summit: The beacon at the top.

ℹ SUPERB SUNSETS
A favourite spot at sunset is Signal Hill. There is no walk involved in this — just continue on Signal Hill Drive to the parking lot at the end and find yourself a spot on the grass looking over the Atlantic seaboard.

Standing proud: Lion's Head dominates the Atlantic seaboard above Camps Bay.

will see, in turn, Sea Point, Robben Island, Table Bay and Blouberg across the bay. At the only fork, keep to the right, heading upwards.

When you're directly above Signal Hill, and just after passing a small "cave", follow the path signposted to your right. This will take you up a steel ladder. The path above the ladder is easy to follow.

When you reach a lone Stone Pine tree on your right, stone steps lead up towards a small cliff face above you. Here you will see the famous Lion's Head chains – not the originals, though – and here you have a choice, as indicated by a sign with arrows. The quickest route is straight up the chains, and they are actually easy to negotiate. Just take things slowly.

Alternatively you can simply carry on along the contour path to the left, which takes you around to a point overlooking Camps Bay where it then leads up a short, easy rock scramble. Once you've negotiated this first scramble, you can continue all the way to the summit along the ridge, but an easier option is, when you reach the first flat open area, to follow the path to the right. This takes you towards a group of Stone Pines where you meet the main path again, but you are now above the chains.

WHAT YOU CAN EXPECT

Distance: about two kilometres one way
Time: an hour to an hour and a half up
Rating: easy with some minor rock scrambling
Children: yes, but may require help at the chains
Dogs: not recommended
Water: none

In full bloom: A hiker on Lion's Head passes a stand of Ursinias in spring.

From the top of the chains, follow the path up, over the slippery roots of one of the Stone Pines and up a short rock scramble. You will now find yourself on the ridge – mind the steep drop straight ahead! Follow the path to the right, all along the ridge, and negotiate one more steel ladder before reaching the summit. A general rule of thumb while going up the ridge is to keep towards the right, rather than heading for the left with its sheer cliffs. The ridge is exposed but it's quite safe, provided you are careful – only those with a serious fear of heights will feel uncomfortable. And the view from the top more than compensates for any discomfort on the way up!

FRIENDS OF LION'S HEAD:
© (021) 434-6453, or on the web **www.friendsoflionshead.org.za**

THE PIPE TRACK WALK ②

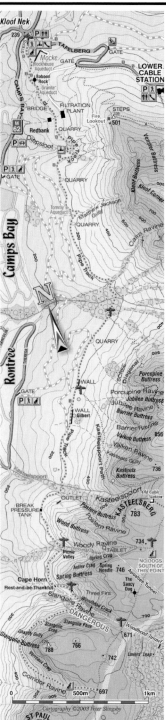

The Pipe Track is precisely what it says: a path constructed to service a pipeline running below the Twelve Apostles. This pipeline was built to carry water from Disa Gorge in Table Mountain's Back Table, via the Woodhead Tunnel through the mountain in Slangolie Ravine, to the Molteno Reservoir in Oranjezicht to help slake the thirst of booming, late 19th century Cape Town.

PROMENADE WITH A VIEW

IN 1888, THE EDITOR of the Cape Argus suggested: "This path (the Pipe Track) ... will be recognised as the promenade of the inhabitants of the suburbs of the future." Promenade is not quite the right word: the path is neither completely level, nor is its surface anywhere smooth. In several places, it is very stony, but it

> **WARNING**
> The Pipe Track is very exposed to the hot afternoon sun in summer; it is at its best early on summer mornings and especially during winter, when many of its protea species are in bloom.

is an easily accessible and popular walk, with many locals making regular use of sections; it is part of Atlantic seaboard's fabric of life.

Atlantic views: Towards Oudekraal, top, and across Camps Bay and Clifton beaches towards Robben Island, below.

Comfortable trail: This path is easily accessible for children and the elderly.

PARK IN THE PARKING AREA on the left at the intersection of Kloof Nek Road and Tafelberg Road. The walk – clearly sign-posted – starts on the opposite side, up a flight of granite stairs leading past a City Council waterworks house and the Mocke reservoir dating from 1896. Almost immediately the path offers the first of a series of superb views of Oudekraal, Bakoven, Camps Bay and Clifton, and you will soon see the pipeline that gives it its name. There are still several Stone Pines (*Pinus pinea*) here – although an alien plant species, these pines have been spared because they are recognised as part of the city's cultural landscape, and they do offer welcome shade. Most of the open land below the Pipe Track between Camps Bay and Llandudno is still privately owned and parts are infested with invasive alien plants. But in the Park's section, there is near pristine fynbos with many mature proteas, including big specimens of "tree" proteas and protea shrubs: Kreupelhout or Tree Pincushion (Gnarled Wood) (*Leucospermum conocarpodendron*), Common Sugarbush (*Protea repens*), Black-beard Sugarbush (*Protea lepidocarpodendron*) and the Waboom (*P. nitida*) – a wonderful sight in full bloom. The Tree Pagoda (*Mimetes fimbriifolius*) is now very rare here.

After about an hour you pass the start of the Kasteelspoort path, a popular route up the mountain. Five minutes later, your path meets the concrete jeep track coming up from Camps Bay. You will not mistake Slangolie which you reach in about an hour and a half to two hours: there is a long set of steep stone stairs to negotiate, exposed water pipes and, as the sign warns, exposed scree (rocks) on the slopes above that is very dangerous. If you continue to Corridor Ravine, cross Slangolie stream and head up the steep slope on the other side. This path, not well used, is neither easy nor level, but as you come around into Corridor Ravine, there are great views of the Oudekraal coastline below.

WHAT YOU CAN EXPECT

Distance: about 6km one way to Corridor Ravine
Time: about four to four-and-a-half hours return
Rating: easy to Slangolie, moderate to Corridor
Children: yes, but the full route is tough
Dogs: yes
Water: tap at the start; take lots in summer

Cape treasures: The Fire Erica blooms gloriously after a fynbos blaze (left) while March Lilies (right) mark the start of the Cape's autumn.

THROUGH THE MOUNTAIN

Work on the 700m Woodhead Tunnel through the Twelve Apostles started in 1887, and it was formally opened in 1891 by mayor Sir John Woodhead. A small tunnel mined through the shortest route under the Twelve Apostles, it has one slight curve and two pipes which carried the water. Slangolie is very exposed, and periodic rockfalls damaged the pipeline; eventually, it was decided to build a new tunnel. Work began on the 1 300m Apostles Tunnel in 1960 and the final break-through came on 14 October 1961. The tunnel starts 400m north of the Woodhead Tunnel in Disa Gorge and exits below Postern Buttress on the southern flank of Kasteelspoort. The water flows through the tunnel itself, not in a pipe, and it's still in use today.

Rock Kestrel

Up – relentlessly up! That's the only way to describe the path in Platteklip Gorge. It's the most direct route to the top of the mountain (excluding the cableway, of course) and probably the most popular. Because it can get so busy, it's jocularly referred to as "Adderley Street" by long-time hikers, but it is not a route to be trifled with; the going can be tough.

WHAT YOU CAN EXPECT

Distance: about 3km (but distance here is irrelevant)
Time: between one hour for the super-fit to three hours for the slow
Rating: moderate to tough, depending on fitness and weather
Children: older children yes, but it is demanding
Dogs: not recommended, and not on the cableway
Water: always take plenty of your own, especially in summer (▲98)

THE 'HIGHWAY' TO THE TOP

THIS PATH IS WELL CONSTRUCTED with stone steps and anti-erosion gabions (wire baskets filled with rocks), and is not difficult to negotiate at any point. But it is steep, and the best way to tackle Platteklip is slowly – don't try to rush it, and frequent stops will also Watsonia give you a chance to look back at the great view of Cape Town and Table Bay below.

To get to the start, leave your car at the parking area 1.5km past the Lower Cableway Station, opposite a huge retaining wall of gabions. The path starts on a modest incline with a series of big stone steps through a shaded area of Rooiels and other indigenous trees, alongside the stream that becomes a torrent after heavy rain. After 10 to 20 minutes, you will reach Breakfast Rock at the junction with the Contour Path, marked by a signpost – in summer, this is your last chance for any decent shade until you get close to the top, so make the most of this opportunity.

Turn left here, follow the Contour Path for about 100 metres along a very stony section, and then turn right at the next intersection, also clearly

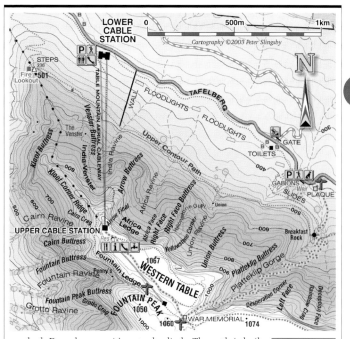

Cartography ©2003 Peter Slingsby

marked. From here on, it's a steady climb. The path is built in a series of zig-zags to make the climb easier, although there are a few steeper sections. Please don't take any of the short-cuts, however tempting they may look – they cause serious erosion.

Eventually the gorge starts narrowing and you get the first welcome confirmation that the end is in sight. Finally, you reach the massive boulders that mark the top, with only a short set of stone steps left to negotiate. This last section of the gorge is dramatic, confirming Peter Mundy's 1634 description: " ... wondrous steep, the rocks on each side like monstrous walls".

At the top of the gorge, turn right for the Upper Cableway Station: the path here is unmistakable, with a series of poles and chains to help the easy ascent up the small rock face at the edge of the Western Table. The path leads directly towards the cableway station. This part of the walk will take about 15 minutes, although it's worth spending longer exploring the 21 excellent interpretive plaques on the network of paths around the cableway station.

Carpet: Post-fire Watsonias on the Front Face of the mountain.

WARNING

Don't underestimate Platteklip Gorge, which can be extremely hot and/or very cold and windy. The temperature at the top can be much lower than on Tafelberg Road, with an icy wind blowing, even in January and February. Always take enough water, a hat, sunblock and warm, windproof clothing with you – even on hot summer days!

GETTING DOWN

Unless you are planning to walk down again – which is tough on the knees! – remember to take money for the cableway (▲94/7). But before setting out on your hike, check that it is in fact operating.

107

Handsome: A Rock Agama in bright breeding colours.

Sun-lovers: Dassies are common at the Upper Cableway Station.

This walk is a must if you want to be able to say you've stood at the highest point on Table Mountain, even if at 1 088m it is only 21m above the Upper Cableway Station. (▲19)

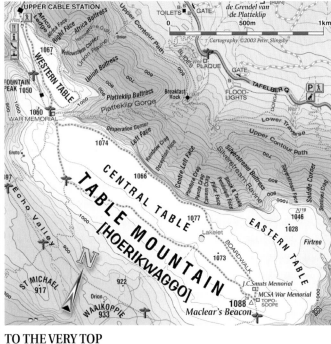

TO THE VERY TOP

FROM THE UPPER CABLEWAY STATION, choose the main path leading to the diagonally opposite corner of what is known as the Western Table – look for interpretive plaques 13 and 14 as guide marks to make sure you're on the right track. It will take you 10 to 15 minutes to walk across to the point where poles and chains have been provided to assist the short climb down the rocky steps at the edge: it is not difficult. Do not attempt to climb down at any other point! At the foot of the chains you will find a signposted intersection: your path goes straight on, up the short rock face leading onto the Central Table. From here, the path to Maclear's Beacon (▲ 19) is marked by painted yellow footprints. Don't be tempted by the footprint pointing left that you see almost immediately: this indicates your return journey.

Keeping dry: Boardwalks over wetland sections on the path.

You soon reach a beacon of packed stones on your left – this is not Maclear's! But from here look to the horizon, just left of the profile of the distant Hottentots Holland mountains across False Bay, and you will see the outline of your beacon, about two kilometres away. The formal cemented path soon ends, but the track is well worn all the way, and watch for the yellow footprints. You pass through several stands of restios (reeds) which signal the marshy, wetland nature of much of the Central Table because of

Maclear's Beacon: The highest point on Table Mountain.

the high precipitation of the "Table Cloth" (▲42/3). Boardwalks help protect the vegetation from trampling in some wetter sections, but in other places the path can be quite muddy. The general low growth of the fynbos is proof of the Central Table's extremely exposed nature: it is constantly buffeted by both south-easterly and north-westerly gales. At the base of the rocky outcrop on which Maclear's Beacon stands – one of the few sheltered spots in this area – is a fine stand of King Proteas.

For the return journey, go slightly past the beacon and climb down into the natural amphitheatre below to the left. The Mountain Club of South Africa holds an annual memorial service here, and it is also home to the Smuts Memorial: a bronze plaque honouring General Jan Smuts (▲20/1). The path back starts on a boardwalk from the amphitheatre, and leads

Abundance: A variety of restios are seen on this walk.

> **WARNING**
> Do not attempt this walk if there is low cloud or mist on the mountain. It is very easy to become disoriented and to lose your way.

through restios and across a wetland area towards the front face of the mountain, where there are some truly spectacular views of the city below. Although the path runs close to the precipitous edge, it is quite safe, and at the only point where you are actually close enough to fall off, should you inadvertently stumble, there is an "inland" alternative. However, those with a serious fear of heights should probably avoid this route; it is also not recommended during strong winds. The path curves inland before you reach the edge of Platteklip Gorge – follow the yellow footprints until you connect up with your outward path and simply retrace your steps to the cableway.

Precipitous: An optional path follows the mountain's Front Face.

> **WHAT YOU CAN EXPECT**
>
> **Distance:** 5.5km overall
> **Time:** 45 minutes to an hour one way to Maclear's Beacon
> **Rating:** easy
> **Children:** yes
> **Dogs:** not recommended
> **Water:** none

CONTOUR PATH: ⑤
KING'S BLOCKHOUSE TO KIRSTENBOSCH

This is a reasonably long walk that will take you through some magnificent Afromontane forest remnants, and it's ideal for summer because most is in shade. It's a one-way route – equally pleasing in either direction – so you'll need to make appropriate transport arrangements at the finish.

ON THE COOL EASTERN SLOPES

START FROM THE RHODES MEMORIAL parking area and head straight up towards the twin peaks above: Devil's Peak and Minor Peak. The King's Blockhouse is clearly visible on the right flank of the latter. This first section is a real slog: the path is badly eroded (but due for reconstruction) and it climbs 250m without respite, but the rest of the walk is definitely worth this initial pain. Some 25 to 35 minutes from the start you will come to a stile★ marking the northern boundary of Rhodes Estate and with lovely views out over the Cape Flats and False Bay. Your Contour Path route to Kirstenbosch starts here, but first take 20 minutes for a quick look at the King's Blockhouse (see box, right). When you've done that, head back and take the upper path on the southern side of the stile to get onto the Contour Path. You'll pass First Waterfall and Second Waterfall ravines – both wild and

DEFENDING THE BLOCKHOUSE

The King's Blockhouse was built by the British between 1795 and 1803. To get there, make your way to the stile★ described at left. On the Cape Town side of the stile, follow the upper jeep track all the way around to the blockhouse – it will take only 10 minutes or so. Alternatively, about 100m from the stile, look for a very steep, log-stepped path among the big Silver Trees which leads from the jeep track. This will take you into the maw of one of the two cannons 'guarding' the blockhouse. You can't enter the blockhouse, which was declared a historical monument in 1936, but enjoy its commanding 270-degree views from Table Bay to False Bay.

WHAT YOU CAN EXPECT

Distance: about 6km
Time: ± two and a half to three hours one way
Rating: easy, shade most of the way
Children: yes, but it is quite tiring
Dogs: yes, on a leash in the Kirstenbosch section
Water: it is recommended that you always take your own

Shady: The Contour Path above Kirstenbosch.

potentially dangerous parts of the mountain, so don't be tempted to stray here. This first section of the walk is still dominated by huge eucalypts and other alien trees, although they're in the process of being removed. This area is a sober reminder of how much work remains to restore the mountain to its indigenous finery. After some 20 to 30 minutes, you go through a second stile and soon reach Newlands Forest; from here it's rich indigenous forest almost all the way to Kirstenbosch. About 20 minutes after the second stile, and 10 minutes after crossing a huge scree field (a jumble of exposed rocks and boulders), you'll reach Ascension Gully – the name is painted on a rock.

Almost immediately after this gully, the path forks – continue right. You'll go through another massive area of scree, pass Hiddingh Ravine and then reach the first sign saying "Welcome to Kirstenbosch". From here, dogs must be on a leash.

But don't head down into Kirstenbosch yet; continue up on the Contour Path. And "up" is the right word, for here a long series of log steps leads 150m up around The Aloes, a wild scree area. And just when you think you've reached the top of the stairs, there are more! But there are lots of forest delights to distract you – like the many colourful mosses, lichens and fungi, and the delicate blue Plectranthus blooms on the forest floor. There are equally steep steps down the other side. At the bottom, you'll find another route back to Kirstenbosch, but rather keep going on the Contour Path; similarly ignore the Yellowwood Trail option here. You'll soon reach Skeleton Gorge waterfall –

Fortress: The King's Blockhouse.

dramatic after heavy rain, and always an entrancing spot. Just after the waterfall you'll meet the Smuts Track and the Yellowwood Trail at a clear junction; this is where you should head down to Kirstenbosch. If you have dogs with you, turn right at the first service road/jeep track you reach: follow this down, turning left just before the big dam, and it will take you to Rycroft Gate – the only entrance or exit for dogs.

111

SKELETON GORGE TO MACLEAR'S BEACON: THE SMUTS TRACK ⑥

Maclear's Beacon
(▲19)

The Smuts Track is one of the most popular walks on Table Mountain, and particularly so in summer because the deep green Afromontane forest offers dappled shade almost all the way up Skeleton Gorge, the toughest section. The climb is steep and unrelenting, although nowhere difficult or requiring more than an ability to climb a wooden ladder and negotiate a few rocky steps. But many people underestimate the effort required, particularly when they go all the way to Maclear's Beacon. Be prepared; don't make the same mistake.

Bush dweller: Speckled Mousebird

COOL IN SUMMER

Delicate: Blue Disa

WHAT YOU CAN EXPECT

Distance: ±4km
Time: From 2 hours for the super-fit to 4 hours for the less-than-fit (one way)
Rating: moderate, no shade in the second half
Children: yes
Dogs: not recommended
Water: mountain streams usually flow, but it's best to take your own (▲98)

A little help: One of the wooden ladders placed in Skeleton Gorge to help hikers.

TECHNICALLY THE SMUTS TRACK starts in Kirstenbosch, but the heart of this route begins at the intersection of Skeleton Gorge and the Contour Path. To reach this point, follow the directions for Walk 7 (▲114/15). Here, a historic bronze plaque marking the Smuts Track was set into a rock where Smuts rested regularly; unfortunately, it was stolen by scrap metal thieves. The first 40 to 75 minutes (depending on your fitness) is spent in the forest, climbing well-constructed log and stone steps. It's tiring, but the beautiful forest surroundings, the peaceful trickle of the stream (except after heavy rain, when it roars) and the chorus of birds (if you start early enough) is more than enough to reward you for the physical effort. And if you think the going is tough, console yourself with the thought that "Oubaas" Smuts was still regularly walking up and down here when well into his 70s. About two thirds of the way up, a series of wooden ladders has been constructed to ease the way over a steep rocky section.

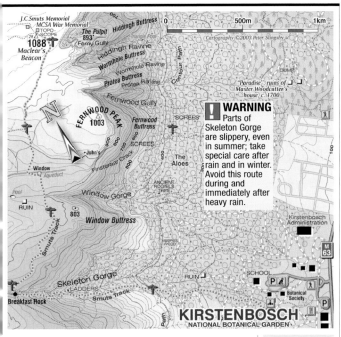

Map labels (clockwise/reading order):

J.C.Smuts Memorial
MCSA War Memorial
TOPO-SCOPE
1088
Maclear's Beacon
The Pulpit 893
Ferny Gully
Hiddingh Buttress
Hiddingh Ravine
Triangle Pool
Wormhole Buttress
Wormhole Ravine
Protea Buttress
Protea Ravine
Fernwood Gully
Contour Path
Cartography ©2003 Peter Slingsby
0   500m   1km
"Paradise" ruins of Master Woodcutter's house, c. 1700
DUMP
FERNWOOD PEAK 1003
Fernwood Buttress
SCREES
John's
Finsteraar Crack
SCREES
The Aloes
ANCIENT ROOIELS TREE
Window Gorge
Window Buttress
803
Aqueduct
Window
Pool
RUIN
Smuts Track
Skeleton Gorge
LADDERS
Breakfast Rock
Smuts Track
RUIN
SCHOOL
P
Kirstenbosch Administration
M 63
Botanical Society
P
KIRSTENBOSCH
NATIONAL BOTANICAL GARDEN

⚠ WARNING Parts of Skeleton Gorge are slippery, even in summer; take special care after rain and in winter. Avoid this route during and immediately after heavy rain.

The top part of the forest narrows, and the path runs over rocks in the stream bed where it's especially slippery. When a big gabion (rock-filled wire basket designed to prevent erosion) blocks your way, head right where the path zig-zags up and out of the stream bed. The path now leaves the forest, climbs a bit more through fynbos, and you will soon reach the unmistakable Breakfast Rock.

Just behind the rock, and signposted, is the path leading right to Maclear's Beacon. It still climbs, but the gradient is much more gentle from here, and the fynbos and views out to the right over the Peninsula and False Bay are excellent.

This section of the walk takes you up three distinct rock bands before reaching Maclear's. The first is just after crossing Window Gorge, where to the left you see the Aqueduct constructed to

Shady path: Afromontane forest dominates most of hike up the gorge.

feed more water to the Hely-Hutchinson dam – a good place to see Red Disas in late summer. A landmark at the second rock band is a huge block of rock resembling a dislodged section of castle ramparts. Just beyond this is a signpost, pointing the way right. After crossing a boardwalk, there's a third minor rock scramble, at the top of which you can see to your left the signpost that is within a few metres of Maclear's Beacon. The views from the beacon itself are somewhat obscured, so first enjoy the astounding views from the rocks on the right overlooking Hiddingh Buttress and "The Pulpit".

There are several options for getting down from Maclear's: via the cableway, Platteklip Gorge (▲106), or simply retrace your steps. If you plan to use any other route, like Nursery Ravine, be sure to have a good map.

NAMED FOR A GENERAL

The path was formally named the General Smuts Track to honour Field Marshall (General) Jan Smuts (1870-1950), the Boer War hero and international statesman who played a leading role in the creation of the United Nations. Smuts was also a philosopher and was twice prime minister of South Africa, including during World War 2. The path has become known simply as the Smuts Track. The path's naming was an honour made just in time in 1950, for the 'Oubaas', as he was popularly known, died the same year, his 80th. A keen mountaineer all his life, this path was a favourite of his (▲ 20).

African Monarch butterfly

113

CONTOUR PATH: KIRSTENBOSCH TO CONSTANTIA NEK ⑦

Mass display: An Erica in full bloom.

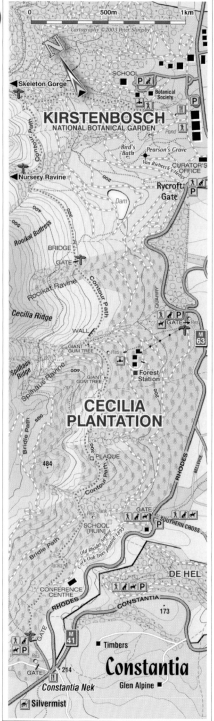

This is a delightful, easy walk offering forest glades, mountain fynbos and superb views over Kirstenbosch and the southern Peninsula. It can be done as a continuation of the Contour Path walk from Rhodes Memorial (▲110/11), which together make for a fairly substantial outing, or as a much shorter walk in its own right. It can also easily be done as a circular route and/or walked in either direction; if you do it as described here, remember to arrange transport back from Constantia Nek.

A SHADY MEANDER

FROM THE KIRSTENBOSCH MAIN ENTRANCE, head for the Smuts Track and Contour Path (▲112). Before you set out buy a copy of the Kirstenbosch guide – a mere R2 (2004 price) – to help you find the way. If you want to take dogs, you must start at the Rycroft Gate, or top gate. The start of Smuts Track is also the beginning of the garden's Yellowwood Trail, opposite the delightful fragrance garden. The route is initially a broad gravel track, bounded on either side by big Wild Almond trees, and soon turns right into a path through the forest. It emerges just above a jeep track. Continue right and you will soon cross another jeep track where there's a sign pointing right to Newlands Forest and left to Constantia Nek. The

latter point is your ultimate destination, but don't take this track now. Instead, continue through the forest. This well-constructed path is steep, so enjoy the tranquil forest at a leisurely pace. Some 30 to 45 minutes after the start of the walk, you will arrive at the easily identifiable intersection of the Contour Path and Skeleton Gorge – this is where you would head up if you were continuing on the Smuts Track (▲112/13). This is a good spot for a rest and to appreciate the many indigenous forest trees. Instead of heading up, turn south along the Contour Path – left if you're facing the mountain – following the sign saying Nursery Ravine/Constantia Nek. After a few minutes, you leave the forest and enter mountain fynbos, dominated by the biggest true proteas, the Waboom (*Protea nitida*). Its name is literally "wagon tree" in Afrikaans, and its wood was used extensively in wagon-making. There are also Silver Trees (▲ 59) which look superficially similar. This section of the walk offers wonderful views of the botanic gardens and out across the Cape Flats.

After about 10 minutes you will find yourself in sylvan Nursery Ravine – also a popular route up Table Mountain. Continue on the Contour Path and at the first intersection after Nursery, keep right. When you reach steps and another intersection, go down on the route marked Constantia Nek/Contour Path, which takes you over the boundary of Kirstenbosch into Cecilia Forest, marked by a line of big gum trees. The path widens to become a jeep track and leads through pine plantations. As you approach Cecilia Ravine, the pines give way to indigenous forest remnants. At a junction, marked by a massive gum tree and a stone wall, take the upper track. At the next intersection, keep heading down, and about five minutes later, at the point where you go down through a boom across the track, keep straight ahead. About 10 minutes after the boom you'll arrive at the forest entrance, some 200m up from Constantia Nek.

WHAT YOU CAN EXPECT

Distance: 6km
Time: about two hours one way
Rating: easy, lots of shade
Children: yes
Dogs: yes, on a leash
Water: at Kirstenbosch. Streams usually flow but it's best to take your own. (▲ 98)

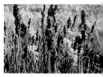

Restios, ericas and sedges

This is another of Cape Town's very popular walks, and with good reason. It's an easy route – okay, there's a lot of uphill on the outward leg, but the path is straightforward – and there are brilliant, undiluted views over the eastern Peninsula and False Bay to enjoy. Then there is wonderful fynbos on the flatish Back Table on top, and the presence of five historic dams with their finely dressed stone walls comes as a big surprise to most first-timers (▲21).

R?
trif

Dry: Victoria Dam on the Back Table holds just a puddle in late summer.

A ROAD WELL TRAVELLED

PARK AT CONSTANTIA NEK and make your way through the gate at the southern entrance to Cecilia Plantation. A well-constructed log path starts almost immediately on your left up through the pine plantation. (You can also go all the way up by staying on the jeep track, also called the Bridle Path – this is longer, but less steep. If you do take this track, keep left at both the next two intersections!)

The path climbs steadily just inside the fringe of the plantation, and you will be in shade here most of the way. It then crosses the jeep track at a "zig-zag" and continues. In this upper section, the path is on the plantation's boundary, and you will only have shade in the morning. Also, some compartments of mature pines in this area were harvested in 2003, and the upper reaches of the path are now open. But the views exposed by the felled pines and the welcome

Cartography ©2003 Peter Slingsby

Top view: Hikers enjoy the splendid view from the bridge at Spilhaus Ravine.

WHAT YOU CAN EXPECT

Distance: about four kilometres
Time: about two hours (one way)
Rating: easy, but uphill! Shade at beginning and end
Children: yes, but tiring
Dogs: yes, on a leash in the top section
Water: untreated from a tap outside the Wynberg overseer's house

opportunity for fynbos to recover more than compensate for the loss of shade. After about 30 to 45 minutes' climb, the path emerges at a concrete track. Turn left here, and the track soon swings right again to start the steepest part of the climb. When you reach the little bridge that crosses Spilhaus Ravine, take a breather and admire the superb views. You'll probably see Red-winged Starlings (*Onychognathus morio*) flying below. The concrete track then continues "inland" and after 10 minutes you pass De Villiers Dam and soon reach the house formerly occupied by the Wynberg dams overseer. Here a tap gives untreated, but safe, drinking water.

The track continues to climb, past Alexandra and then Victoria Dams on the right, and spectacular fynbos

No change: The lower sections of Cecilia Forest will be retained as commercial pine plantations in the medium-to-long term, with all the existing recreational opportunities still available.

marked by particularly chunky restios on the left. Higher on the right are the remains of pine trees: much of the Back Table was under alien pines before they were sensibly removed during the 1970s and '80s. Before long, you will overlook Woodhead Reservoir, where there is shade under the few remaining pines. Just to to the north you'll see the wall of Hely-Hutchinson Reservoir. This walk ends here, but it's easy to follow the jeep track around in front of Hely-Hutchinson, past the Waterworks Museum (▲21 for details of opening hours) and then past another overseer's house and back again over the wall of Woodhead to complete the circle. To get home, retrace your steps.

! WARNING
There are many walking routes leading from Woodhead Reservoir, including one which takes you most directly to the Upper Cableway Station. But this latter walk involves crossing a sizeable ridge, then a valley and another steep climb, and it will probably take another two hours. The easier option to get to the cableway from Woodhead is via Maclear's Beacon on the Smuts Track. If you're planning to do this, make sure you have a map.

Cape Skink

Dragonfly

Easy going:
Marshy areas have
been made easier
to traverse with a
fine boardwalk.

WHAT YOU CAN EXPECT

Distance: about
2km one way
Time: 45
minutes to one
hour
Rating: easy, lots
of shade
Children: yes
Dogs: yes
Water: from the
river in winter
and spring, but
it's best to take
your own (▲ 98)

The Silvermine River Walk is a short trail
specially constructed to introduce people to
the pleasures of the river and its riverine
vegetation, although it doesn't
stay right next to the actual
watercourse all the way.

**Fynbos
delight:**
*Saltera
sarcocolla*

MEANDERING WITH THE RIVER

WELL-CONSTRUCTED BOARDWALKS have been built
through particularly wet or marshy sections, and while
there are one or two places where you clamber over
some very short rocky outcrops, this path is well within
the capabilities of just about everyone, young or old.
The trail can be walked in either direction and is in fact
short enough to do easily as an "out and back" without
much effort. Alternatively, if you do the "out" walk – up
the river – you can send some of your family/group
ahead by road to prepare the braai at the popular
Silvermine Dam picnic site – where this
trail ends – or simply continue with one
of several other possible walks from the
end point.

Drive up Ou Kaapse Weg from the Cape
Town side and just before the top, turn
right to get to the main entrance to the
Silvermine section of the Park: one of
only four pay points in the Park.
After paying, make an immediate left
turn and park in the grassy parking area.
Walk down the gravel road, admiring
here the rapid recovery of fynbos
following the removal of pine trees in
2000. Turn right at the sign saying
"Silvermine River Walk" and stay on the
gravel track, taking its left-hand fork. It
ends at a boardwalk crossing the river at

**GETTING
THERE**
Silvermine
is one of the
Park's pay areas.
The cost (2004
prices) is R10 for
adults and R5 for
scholars and
pensioners.
A much better,
and of course
much cheaper,
alternative is to
make sure you
have a WILD
Card which will
give you free
entry. (▲ 6)

the start of the trail. On either side you will see the stout
Palmiet reeds (*Prionium serratum*) which are a major
feature of this walk. Palmiet, which has an extremely
tough root system, creates dense mats or barriers in
rivers like the Silvermine, acting as a natural flood

Under a canopy:
A dense stand of
young Keurbooms
(*Virgilia* sp).

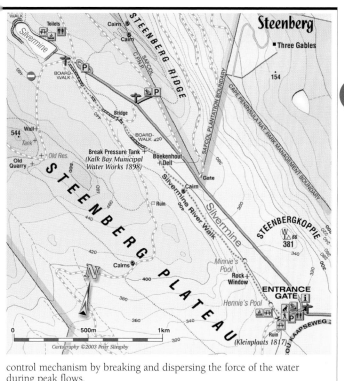

Steenberg
■ Three Gables

control mechanism by breaking and dispersing the force of the water during peak flows.

Initially the path is a sandy track slightly away from the river. Here you will find several exquisite Erica species and the pink flower of *Saltera sarcocolla*, sitting a-top its curiously precise geometric arrangement of leaves. This is one of six plant families endemic to fynbos.

A *Virgilia* (Keurboom) species has returned with such profusion following the big fire that swept through this part of the Park in January 2000, that in places on the trail you literally walk through a tunnel of these young trees. But they are pioneer plants – a pioneer species is a relatively short-lived one which recolonises a disturbed area first and helps recreate a suitable habitat for longer-lived plants – and will not last too long in this form.

After about 25 or 30 minutes you reach the first really accessible pool at the river: Minnie's Pool, marked by a big Rooiels tree and Palmiet reeds. Then 10 minutes later you come to the small waterfall at Boekenhout Dell – a delightful little spot where you will need to do some very minor boulder-hopping as you cross the river. This is followed by more boardwalks through dense stands of Palmiet – don't be tempted to touch them because they have razor-sharp edges!

After about 40 or 45 minutes you will cross a gravel track, and bear marginally left to continue on the last section of the walk, which also has boardwalk sections. The walk ends at the jeep track just below the Silvermine Dam wall; turn right for the car park or left for a delightful walk around the dam.

Secret charms: A step onto the river bank will reveal hidden delights.

Golden display: Daisies provide a burst of colour near the start of this walk.

Silvermine River Walk

119

SILVERMINE TO NOORDHOEK PEAK WALK (10)

Leucadendron

This is an easy walk, mostly on a gravel jeep track, and if you decide to add in Elephant's Eye Cave as well, you will traverse three superb viewpoints that together offer a 360-degree panoramic sweep of the Peninsula: south to Clovelly, Fish Hoek, Noordhoek and Kommetjie; west over Hout Bay and Karbonkelberg; north to the Back Table of Table Mountain, Devil's Peak and Constantia; and east across the southern Peninsula taking in Steenberg, Tokai and Muizenberg and across False Bay. It takes some beating!

SPECTACULAR VIEWS IN EVERY DIRECTION

Eye on the world: At the Elephant's Eye Cave.

THIS WALK STARTS FROM THE CAR PARK at Silvermine Dam. Follow the gravel track below the reservoir wall which swings slightly left on the southern bank. This is a good place to observe the miracle of fynbos recovery: pine forests stood on either side of this track into the late 1990s.

The gravel track climbs steeply, and soon you reach a branch leading off left to the now demolished fire look-out. This is worth a quick detour for the views, but mind the drop – the cliff-face is precipitous! Continue up – the track is still steep here – and you will soon pass through a lovely little wetland area marked by the clicking of frogs among the restios. This is a good place to find spectacular long-tubed Painted Ladies (*Gladiolus angustus*) and the lovely *Disa racemosa* after fire. In fact, all the fynbos on this walk is spectacular, and it offers a particularly

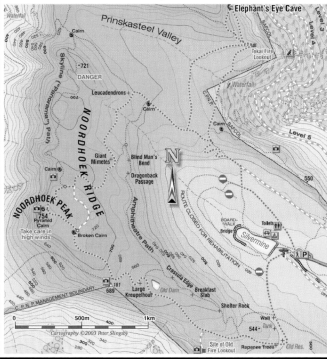

Cartography: ©2003 Peter Slingsby

Dazzling colours: Lichen growing on a rock.

Breath-taking: The view of the Sentinel from Noordhoek Peak.

good opportunity to brush up on your Ericas – you will easily find a half-dozen different species within the space of just a few metres.

After three sharp zig-zags, a path leads left towards a beacon: this short detour offers wonderful views south over the Noordhoek Valley, Chapman's Peak, and the extensive beach and wetlands towards Kommetjie.

Continue on the jeep track and after a few hundred metres, when it has levelled out, look for a well-worn sandy path leading off left. Follow this and you will soon see the beacon on top of Noordhoek Peak, a little way in front of you.

Once at the beacon, leave enough time to enjoy one of the finest views on the Peninsula: of Chapman's Peak Drive, Hout Bay, its famous Sentinel, Karbonkelberg, Little Lion's Head and Judas Peak. You will be reluctant to drag yourself away, especially on a clear day, when the shallow coastal water sparkles aquamarine in the foreground.

When leaving, keep left along an eroded path, and you will soon meet the jeep track again. The easiest walking is along this track, but there's a very pleasant, if slightly overgrown, path off to the right about 400m down – it meets up with the track again about a kilometre further on. The whole area is a great place to see the magnificent King Protea (*Protea cynaroides*) blooming during autumn.

Before the jeep track becomes a concrete strip road, a branch of the track leads left; this is the way to Elephant's Eye Cave. Follow the branch for about a kilometre to a fire lookout hut (still in use), which is the third excellent vantage point of this walk. From here, the cave is clearly visible above you. Although its entrance is impressive – it forms the "eye" in the "elephant" shape of Constantiaberg as seen from below in Tokai – it only extends about

Fynbos variety: King Protea and Red Crassula are among the myriad plants seen here.

10 metres into the mountain, but it frames False Bay beautifully.

Retrace your steps to the lookout hut, and then follow the clear path along the edge of the pine trees marking the border with Tokai forest back to the jeep track. This path passes through some thick restios before crossing the small Prinskasteel stream – this section can be very wet in winter. Once back on the jeep track, follow the zig-zags back down to Silvermine.

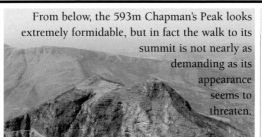

Floral delights
Left and middle, two
species of everlastings
and an *Erica*

From below, the 593m Chapman's Peak looks extremely formidable, but in fact the walk to its summit is not nearly as demanding as its appearance seems to threaten.

WHAT YOU CAN EXPECT

Distance: about 2.5km
Time: 75 to 90 minutes one way
Rating: easy to moderate
Children: yes
Dogs: yes
Water: none

WHERE THE REWARD FAR OUTWEIGHS THE EFFORT

Splendid heaths:
Two common but beautiful *Erica* species:
E.mammosa, above, and *E.coccinea*, below.

GETTING THERE
Travel along Chapman's Peak Drive from Hout Bay to a point about 700m before Lookout Point, and park in the small parking area on the mountain side. The path up is exposed, with no shade, and is best avoided on hot summer afternoons.

THE "MODERATE" PART of this walk's rating (as given above) relates more to the slippery, stony quality of much of the path, than to the physical effort involved in walking here. However, this footpath is earmarked for reconstruction, following the rehabilitation of Chapman's Peak Drive which reopened in December 2003 after a four-year closure. Its outstanding views and modest distance make it an extremely rewarding outing.

Drive up from Hout Bay and park at the car park on a bend of Chapman's Peak Drive, about 700m before the major lookout point at the Drive's highest point. The path starts here. After climbing for 15 to 30 minutes, depending on your state of fitness, you will arrive at a crossroads on the plateau between Noordhoek Peak and Chapman's Peak. Turn right here, and follow the path as it skirts the right-hand shoulder of the 547m Lower Chapman's Peak. Here, the (unreconstructed) path is stony and the going slow, but the deep booming of the surf crashing at the base of the Chapman's Peak cliffs far

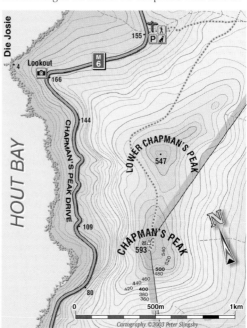

Cartography ©2003 Peter Slingsby

Vantage point: A hiker looks across from Silvermine to the twin summits of Chapman's Peak and Little Chapman's Peak.

Vista: Noordhoek Beach viewed from Chapman's Peak. (▲128/29)

A NAVAL MAN LEFT HIS MARK

Chapman's Peak is named after John Chapman, mate on the British ship Consent which was becalmed off the cliffs of what is now called the Sentinel in July 1607. Sent ashore to check, he was able to report the presence of fresh water and what appeared to be safe anchorage in the bay just around the corner, now called Hout Bay. Subsequent charts referred to the bay as 'Chapman's Chaunce' and it was only after the arrival of Jan van Riebeeck in 1652 that it became Hout Bay (Wood Bay), named for its rich forests. However, the mountain has retained Chapman's name to this day.

below will help take your mind off the climb. To your right, there's the superb sight of the Sentinel guarding the entrance to Hout Bay, and beyond that the rugged, untamed rocky coastline of Karbonkelberg.

About 25 to 30 minutes after the crossroads, you round a corner and Chapman's Peak proper suddenly pops up in front of you, no longer looking nearly as formidable, and the incline eases noticeably as you make your way across the small saddle area between the two peaks. Just before starting the final ascent of the peak, take a two-minute detour to your left along another path which leads to a point overlooking the Noordhoek amphitheatre and the gaping open pit of the kaolin mine (▲28/9) directly below you. The views here are excellent – apart from the mine, of course.

Get back onto the main path, and tackle the remaining few minutes' walk to the peak. The last few metres are a bit of a scramble, and it's easiest to bear left just before the top and go around and then up from the south-eastern side, otherwise you will need to do some very minor scrambling over the big boulders that form the actual summit. But either way, the views all around from the top are simply unbeatable. And to make the most of what is arguably the best of all – out over Noordhoek Beach – head down slightly on the southern side.

Virtually the whole of Chapman's Peak was burnt during the huge wildfires of January 2000, and this walk is an excellent place to see post-fire fynbos regeneration, particularly of the many Protea species thriving here.

Puff Adder: Keep a lookout for snakes on hikes.

Glorious cascade: In full flow during winter, by late summer the waterfall is dry.

This is a delightful and very popular little walk that is suitable for the whole family. Apart from the last 100m or so to the actual waterfall, the entire route is negotiable with a sturdy pushchair for the baby. And although it's not flat, the elderly should manage most of it as well without any trouble.

A GENTLE STROLL TO A WINTER CASCADE

DRIVE OVER OU KAAPSE WEG from the Cape Town side and continue past the main entrance to the Silvermine section of the Park on your right. About 500m further on, after the bend, take the entrance on the left – watch out, because it comes up suddenly. Park here in the newly developed pay parking area (R5 in 2004). Start the walk by taking the right fork of the jeep track just below the imposing Wolfkop outcrop.

WHAT YOU CAN EXPECT

Distance: 2km
Time: 20 to 30 minutes one way
Rating: very easy, no shade except at the waterfall
Children: yes
Dogs: yes
Water: from the river in winter, spring and early summer but it's best to take your own (▲ 98)

Jeep track: The route to the waterfall is popular with families and joggers.

This is another excellent place to see how fynbos flourishes after fire: marvel at the profusion of proteas – particularly the mimetes, pincushions and leucadendrons, the last of which carpet the area in yellowy-green in spring – ericas, everlastings, watsonias, pelargoniums and a host of other species. It's difficult to believe it looked like a wasteland after big blazes in 1999 and 2000. There are large boulders for the kids to scramble on and lots of entrancingly shaped "monkey

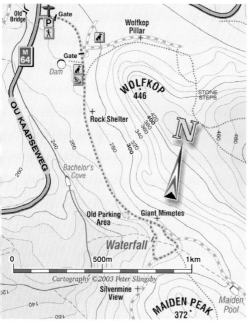

Although there are several species of indigenous trees in the little patch of Afromontane forest at the waterfall, it is dominated by the Rooiels (*Cunonia capensis*), or Red Alder in English, although no-one calls it this. The Rooiels flowers in autumn, with cream-coloured flowers on long stalks. Found wherever water is abundant, it's easy to identify because its leaf buds are enclosed in a distinctive spoon-shaped sheath that opens as the new leaves develop, giving it a common English name: the Butterspoon Tree.

WARNING

Take extra care when turning out from the parking area back into Ou Kaapse Weg. Vehicles often speed on this road, and the exit from the parking area is on a virtual blind bend for motorists travelling from Cape Town.

puzzle" rocks to remind you of the amazing power of wind and water erosion. It's also an excellent place to see Orange-breasted Sunbird.

Just after the summit of a short but steep little hill which you reach about 15 or 20 minutes after setting out, you'll see the sandy path to the waterfall leading off down to the right. At this point you may want to send the youngest and the oldest in your party on to meet you at the other side of the waterfall; tell them to continue on the jeep track, keep right at the fork after about 200m, and then to wait for you at the little bridge about five minutes' walk further on.

The path leading down to the waterfall is sandy with log steps, and it branches about half way at a broad rocky ledge. Head left along this ledge and you'll soon find yourself at the top of the waterfall, which is very dramatic after heavy rain in winter and generally dry from about mid-summer. *Take care close to the edge, particularly when it's wet and slippery: there's a 30m precipitous drop!* The path continues about 10m above the top of waterfall, and brings you out on the jeep track close to the bridge mentioned above – it's about

Changing season: Autumn mist hangs in the valleys in the Silvermine area.

100m to your left. But before you do that, take the lower fork of the path leading to the base of the waterfall. This section is somewhat eroded, but still easy to negotiate. Here is a truly lovely little glade created by some big Rooiels trees, making a cool and wonderful spot for tea in summer. In winter it can be dramatic and you're likely to get exceedingly wet from the spray. Return to the top of the waterfall and now take the path to the jeep track and the bridge.

Fynbos beauties: White everlastings Pelargoniums Leucadendrons.

Watsonia

Centuries old:
Ancient tree trunks are twisted and gnarled.

WHAT YOU CAN EXPECT

Distance: ±6km
Time: about 3 to 4 hours, depending on how long you linger in the forests
Rating: moderate, lots of shade in the forests
Children: yes
Dogs: yes
Water: always at Weary Willy's, but it's best to take your own (▲ 98)

ENCHANTED FORESTS

THE WALK STARTS AT THE OU KRAAL SIGN, marked by a clump of mature indigenous trees, opposite a sharp bend on Boyes Drive above St James. Ignore the steps going straight up, and instead take the stony left-hand path which has a much gentler incline. Start slowly and enjoy the magnificent sweep of False Bay and the sight of the surfers working the Kalk Bay reefs below. If you're walking around midday, you may see the fishing boats heading back to Kalk Bay harbour to offload their catch, flocks of anxious seagulls in their wakes.

After 25 to 35 minutes, you will reach a junction,

Hidden away: The Spes Bona forest lies in a small valley above Kalk Bay.

opposite some rock shelters. Head right, ignoring several inviting short-cuts (they cause erosion). The path changes into a gravel jeep track, and just where this track levels off, look for a wide, sandy-stony path heading left up Spes Bona Valley. You're on the right track when you soon reach a small stone cairn. About an hour after setting out, you enter Spes Bona forest – an absolutely enchanting forest of old, gnarled indigenous trees like the Real Yellowwood (*Podocarpus latifolius*), Assegai (*Curtisia dentata*) and Cape Beech or Boekenhout (*Rapanea melanophloeos*), growing around, over and sometimes even apparently through giant boulders which came crashing down from the cliffs. These boulders provided shelter from fire for the forest saplings; now, the forest is sufficiently robust to survive even major fires. Trees on the margins do get singed or burnt, but fire cannot penetrate into the forest's heart. Walk here in late March and early April and you will find numerous April Fool Flowers (*Haemanthus coccineus*) flowering in the

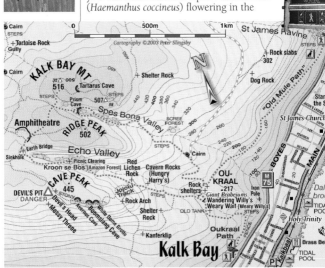

Magic of the forest: Hikers enjoy the cool dappled light of Spes Bona.

forest – hence the name. Out of the forest shade are healthy populations of the spectacular King Protea (*Protea cynaroides*) and Cluster Disa (*Disa ferruginea*). There are also lovely restios, and a sheer cliff on the right as you emerge from the forest is a glistening moss wall. At the top of the valley, look behind you: the valley walls neatly frame Cape Hangklip across False Bay. At the four-way intersection here, turn left; go up the ridge, and then keep right, heading for the Amphitheatre. Don't walk straight on – there's a precipitous drop ahead into Echo Valley! The obvious Amphitheatre, which offers several shady nooks for tea, is a popular cavers' meeting point; *don't* be tempted into any caves without proper equipment and an experienced guide (▲ 146/7).

Mountain stroll: An aerial view of most of this spectacular walk

Head across the Amphitheatre, down past a sinkhole and turn left into Echo Valley where you almost immediately enter another enchanting forest: Kroon se Bos, also called Amazon Forest. Once out of the forest, continue down past the quaintly named Hungry Harry's, or Cavern Rocks, to the intersection and small weir at the equally oddly named Wandering Willy's Weary Wait – Weary Willy's for short (▲ 146/7). Turn left here; if you go right you also emerge on Boyes Drive, but further down towards Kalk Bay. Going left takes you to the intersection opposite the rock shelters where you came up earlier.

ing Bird
Moth

MIMIC IN THE FYNBOS

Floral mimicry, in which one plant imitates another, is unusual in fynbos, but the Cluster Disa (*Disa ferruginea*) is a master. It does not itself produce nectar, so in order to attract a pollinator – in this case, the Table Mountain Beauty (*Aeropetes tulbaghia*), which is attracted to red objects – it has evolved to closely resemble another red flowering plant, *Tritoniopsis triticea*, which produces large amounts of nectar. The insect is 'fooled' into visiting the disa; by the time it realises there's no nectar, it already has the disa's pollen packets – called pollinaria – stuck to its legs and thorax. These will be deposited on another disa to effect pollination.

Distinctive: Th[e]
African Blac[k]
Oystercatche[r]
can b[e]
see[n]
[on]
this wal[k]

KOMMETJIE/NOORDHOEK BEACH WALK ⑭

If you want a real sense of what the wild Cape Peninsula must have been like before the arrival of the European settlers, try this beach walk. Although you're never completely out of sight of human habitation, the booming crash of the huge

Atlantic rollers and the plaintive "klee-wheep" of African Black Oystercatchers drown out any sound of "civilisation".

Particularly at the mid-point of this walk, you're seemingly alone in a coastal

Three-spot Swimming Crab

Wreck: The rusty remains of the Kakapo

wilderness, totally surrounded by sea, beach and hummocky sand dunes; and the forlorn remains of the wreck of the Kakapo (▲ 26/7) add to your sense of glorious isolation. During winter, storm surges coinciding with spring high tides drive the sea over the steep frontal beach area, creating vast, shallow salt-water lagoons that can last for weeks at a time, much to the delight of wading birds.

Open space: Perfect for horse riding.

A WALK ON THE WILD SIDE

THERE ARE SEVERAL POSSIBLE PERMUTATIONS of this walk, but unless you're happy to do an "out-and-back", you'll need to leave a car at the far end. You can walk either way but starting at Kommetjie and walking north has the advantage of majestic views – Chapman's Peak at the far end, flanked by the Sentinel guarding Hout Bay, and the Back Table of Table Mountain in the distance. Also, if the infamous south-easterly is blowing (▲ 42/3), the wind will be at your back. The walk starts at Kommetjie's Long Beach, either from Surf Way or from the parking area in Wireless Road – a better option offering more parking and better ablutions. From either parking area,

simply walk onto the beach and turn right.

Don't be put off by the washed-up kelp (seaweed), at the northern end of Long Beach: it has a pungent odour but is at the heart of an active beach ecosystem. You may see a flock of African Sacred Ibis poking about in the beach debris, as well as several other birds like the Kelp Gull, Hartlaub's Gull, African Black Oystercatcher, Blacksmith Lapwing, White-fronted Plover and Little Egret.

At the end of Long Beach is the rocky point of Klein Slangkop. Although the Kommetjie side of this point has been developed, the northern section has been purchased by SA National Parks, ensuring the conservation integrity of the Noordhoek beach system and its associated wetlands (▲61). Cross the outlet of the Wildevoëlvlei system – you may need to wade in winter – and you're onto Noordhoek beach proper, some 4km of pristine white sand. The wreck of the Kakapo, which in a highly embarrassing moment in May 1900 steamed straight onto the shore, is clearly visible about a kilometre ahead. This walk is nicest at

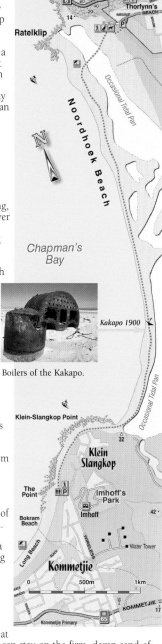

Boilers of the Kakapo.

low tide when you can stay on the firm, damp sand of the inter-tidal area. The walk ends at the dramatic granite boulders of Ratelklip, directly below Chapman's Peak Drive – a fine place for a picnic or a sundowner.

WHAT YOU CAN EXPECT

Distance: about five and a half kilometres
Time: about two hours (one way)
Rating: easy, but no shade
Children: yes
Dogs: yes
Water: taps at both ends

Flotsam: Bladder Kelp, washed up on the beach, is one of the least common West Coast kelps.

STARTING AT NOORDHOEK

Drive through Noordhoek in the direction of Chapman's Peak Drive. Just before the Drive begins, turn left at Avonrust Crescent. Then right into Beach Road and follow the signs to the beach parking area. (Avonrust Circle will also gets you there, although now you will turn left into Beach Road.)
● If you begin at Noordhoek you could walk to the Kakapo wreck and back – about 6km in all.

⚠ WARNING:
Partly because of its isolation, there have been several muggings on Noordhoek beach. National Park staff recommend that people walk in groups, not carry valuables, and report immediately any suspicious behaviour. Phone the police at 10111 or 107.

SIRKELSVLEI WALK (15)

Orange-breasted Sunbird, below, and Angulate Tortoise, right.

Ignore for a moment the sharpish 10-minute climb at the start of this walk which gets you up to the "escarpment" of Smitswinkel Flats, and you have the prospect of a delightful, three-hour, level stroll that will take you through some of the best fynbos anywhere in the Cape of Good Hope section of the Park.

Restio

CIRCULAR SPLENDOUR

SEEING IS BELIEVING

Olifantsbos is believed to be mistakenly named for the rounded shape of the mature fynbos trees of the area: the Kreupelhout or Tree Pincushion (Gnarled Wood) protea, the Tree Pagoda and the Milkwood, which passing sailors mistook for real elephants. The last elephants in the Peninsula were recorded in 1620, before the arrival of the European settlers.

WHILE FIRE CAN CHANGE THINGS OVERNIGHT, around Sirkelsvlei itself you will probably still find superb examples of mature fynbos "trees": the Kreupelhout or Tree Pincushion (Gnarled Wood) protea (*Leucospermum conocarpodendron*) with its bright yellow flowers and the Tree Pagoda (*Mimetes fimbriifolius*) with its pinky-red and cream inflorescence. Bird lovers will rejoice in the lovely sunbirds: these include the endemic Orange-breasted Sunbird and the male Malachite Sunbird with its impossibly iridescent breeding plumage.

Park at Olifantsbos parking area and walk back to the boom where a sign indicates the start of the circular walk which can be done in either direction.

If you take the left fork, going clockwise, you will head up to the tumble of Window Rocks with good views over the small valley known as Die Kloof. But if you choose to go right, the path will first take you past the ruins of the World War 2 "Bosch" submarine look-out post with its fine views north to Slangkop lighthouse and south to the Hoek van Bobbejaan. Then keep left at the intersection where the circular Shipwreck Trail joins. A few minutes after this point, make sure you look left: on a clear day, you will see the unmistakable flat outline of Table Mountain's

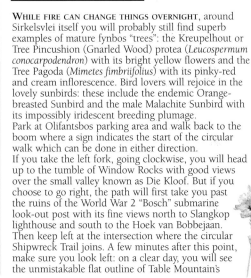

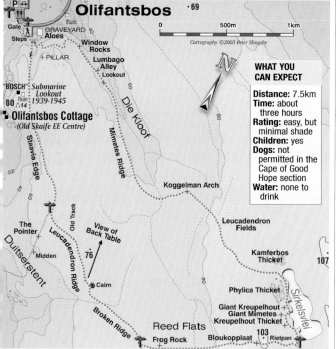

Olifantsbos · 69

Cartography ©2003 Peter Slingsby

0 — 500m — 1km

P
Gate
Steps
GRAVEYARD
Aloes
Window Rocks
PILLAR
Lumbago Alley
Lookout
"BOSCH" Submarine Lookout
Ruin 1939-1945
80
Ruin △14
■ Olifantsbos Cottage
(Old Skaife EE Centre)
Slaavia Edge
Old Track
Die Kloof
Mimetes Ridge
Koggelman Arch
Leucadendron Fields
The Pointer
Leucadendron Ridge
View of Back Table
Duitsestent
Midden
76
Cairn
Kamferbos Thicket
107
Phylica Thicket
Broken Ridge
Reed Flats
Frog Rock
Giant Kreupelhout
Giant Mimetes
Kreupelhout Thicket
Bloukopplaat
103
Rietpan
Sirkelsvlei

WHAT YOU CAN EXPECT

Distance: 7.5km
Time: about three hours
Rating: easy, but minimal shade
Children: yes
Dogs: not permitted in the Cape of Good Hope section
Water: none to drink

Back Table. Keep left again at the next intersection, where the overnight trail joins. Here you may see Red Hartebeest, which have been reintroduced after an absence of many years.

As you cross the wide open Reed Flats and approach Sirkelsvlei, you have a strong sense of the real Cape of Good Hope essence: wild, untamed, wind-swept, and full of magnificent fynbos. At Sirkelsvlei you may see the occasional Spur-winged or Egyptian Goose, but the chemical characteristics of the water limit the food chain, making it unattractive

Red Hartebeest

for birds. However, you will see terrapins (▲77) here. On the way back to Olifantsbos there are dense stands of leucadendrons – Geelbos (*Leucadendron laureolum*) – which turn a bright golden yellow (male plants) and yellowy-green (females) in winter. In a delightful capriciousness on the part of the path builders, the trail leads through the Koggelman rock arch – unnecessary, but a nice touch that kids especially will enjoy.

ℹ HIDDEN SUPPLY

Sirkelsvlei is the largest body of fresh water in the Cape of Good Hope section of the Park, extending over more than six hectares. About 1.4m at its deepest point, it has been known to dry out very occasionally after a dry winter and long hot summer. It's unusual in that there is no obvious inlet and it has only a tiny catchment area. It is probably fed by underground springs.

A TALE OF TWO LIGHTHOUSES

Free-standing:
This dramatic rock pinnacle stands close to the New Lighthouse.

ONE OF THE EARLY SIGNS erected to guide visitors down the "spine walk" path between the Old and New Lighthouses at Cape Point mistakenly suggests that this walk is dangerous and will take one and a half hours for the return trip; neither is correct The path is not at all dangerous – it's not even risky, provided you stick to the demarcated area and don't do anything rash like climbing over the parapet. It is, however, quite steep near the start and gives an illusion of being more exposed than it actually is, particularly when the wind is blowing strongly – as it so often does at Cape Point. And even allowing for a generous amount of time to ➤

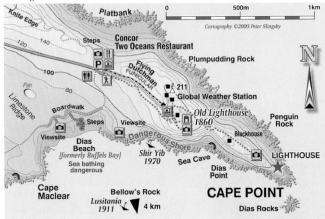

WARNING TO SAILORS: THE OLD AND THE NEW

Cape Point is a prominent navigational landmark, but it has always been hazardous to ships, especially at night. Particular dangers are the menacing presence of Bellows Rock, four kilometres south of the Point and frequently seen breaking, and nearby Anvil Rock. The original lighthouse – now the Old Lighthouse (pictured below) – was commissioned on 1 May 1860, and immediately proved to be a failure. At 238m above sea level, it was situated far too high – its 2 000 candlepower light was frequently obscured by the low fog, mist and cloud often present at the Point. One of the most prominent shipwrecks after its installation was the Portuguese liner Lusitania which struck Bellows Rock at midnight on 18 April 1911 with 800 people aboard (not to be confused with the ship of the same name which was torpedoed by the Germans off Ireland in 1915, early in World War 1). Reports of the number of casualties vary, but the loss of

life was miraculously low – fewer than 10, even though the ship went down soon afterwards. Its loss was a primary motivation for a new lighthouse, construction of which started in 1913.

The site chosen for this second light was much closer to the tip of Cape Point, at a height of just 87m above the water. Construction was difficult and slow, and the New Lighthouse (pictured above) was only lit for the first time at sunset on 11 March 1919. Its original light was a paraffin vapour mantle of 500 000 candlepower, but it was electrified in 1936 and now has an intensity of 10 million candlepower – still the most powerful light on the South African coastline. It gives a group of three flashes every 30 seconds over a nominal range of 34 nautical miles, or 63 kilometres.

The very tip: The narrow promontory that leads to the New Lighthouse.

➤ wonder at the incredible cliff landscape around you, you probably won't take more than an hour overall. This walk, which offers spectacular and easily accessible scenery, starts from behind the upper funicular station, north (inland) of the Global Atmosphere Watch Station. It descends steeply on the False Bay side of the cliffs below the Old Lighthouse, but levels out relatively soon to cross the narrowest part of the promontory. You may feel slightly exposed here, but rope barriers provide more than adequate safety. Observation points with stout stone walls have been built on either side, offering superb views of the towering cliffs above – 200m at their highest – and below. Continue down, passing ugly old buildings dating from World War 2 – most being demolished – to the viewing point directly above the New Lighthouse on its dramatic rocky foundations. There are often vast numbers of seabirds off Cape Point, floating in rafts or flying in strings, making an unforgettable sight. You are also likely to see whales in spring and early summer, as well as Cape Fur Seals and possibly also dolphins (▲90/1).

WHAT YOU CAN EXPECT

Distance: one kilometre one way
Time: about one hour return
Rating: easy, unless you have a serious fear of heights
Children: yes, but keep a close eye on them
Dogs: not permitted in the Cape of Good Hope section
Water: no, but unnecessary unless it's exceptionally hot

⚠ **TAKE CARE IN HIGH WINDS**

CORMORANT TERRITORY

You should see four species of cormorant roosting on the sheer cliff faces, of which two – the easily identifiable White-breasted Cormorant and the smaller Cape Cormorant with its bright orange throat – also breed here. The other two are the all-black Bank Cormorant and the small Crowned Cormorant, both non-breeding visitors. Out to sea you should probably spot numerous Cape Gannet with their sparkling white plumage, and with binoculars you may also identify albatrosses, petrels and prions.

⚠ **DON'T FORGET**
Remember to take binoculars for a close-up view of the numerous seabirds roosting on the cliffs and feeding and swimming in the waters below.

CAPE OF GOOD HOPE HIKING TRAIL

Hikers' delight: The view out over False Bay from near the summit of Da Gama Peak.

The best way to experience the spectacular fynbos of the Park is "up close and personal", and the two-day Cape of Good Hope hiking trail offers a great opportunity to do just that in combination with some of the most breath-taking views on offer anywhere in the Cape Peninsula. The position of the three overnight huts, perched high on the north-facing slopes of the 266m Da Gama Peak, makes them among the most spectacular of their kind anywhere in the world, commanding a vantage point over two oceans: Indian and Atlantic (there is debate over where the oceans meet ▲86) and offering both sunrises and sunsets.

TWO DAYS IN PARADISE

THIS WAS THE FIRST overnight trail developed in the Park.

The trail starts at the main entrance gate to the Cape of Good Hope section of the Park, where you can leave your car. Show your booking reference number here and collect the keys for the overnight hut. It is recommended that you walk this trail in a clockwise direction, partly because you will be better sheltered (but never entirely!) when walking into the prevailing south-easterly wind which is often very strong in summer. On Day Two, this wind will be at your back. Also, the views south to Cape Point along the False Bay coastline are, arguably, even more dramatic than those looking northwards.

Gladiolus maculatus

Highlights of this trail include:
- the gloriously scenic, if slightly dizzying, ramble along the high rim of False Bay on Paulsberg, Die Boer and Judas Peak, with awesome views down to the coast;
- walking among many of the 26 species of the Protea family found in this section of the Park, like the Black-beard Sugarbush (*Protea*

WHEN IT'S TIME TO SLEEP

The Erica hut, which sleeps six, and the nearby observation point – disguised with a fake stone facade (below) – were built during World War 2 (1939-45) and formed the anti-submarine "Diaz Point" observation post manned by members of the 2nd Heavy Battery of Simon's Town Command, watching for German U-boats. This was one of several similar observation posts on the Peninsula; another was at Olifantsbos. The Restio and Protea huts, also each sleeping six, and the buildings on the summit of Da Gama Peak (266m) were used by 61 Coastal Defence Corps during the top-secret development of South Africa's first radar during WW2.

■ The overnight huts are equipped with hot and cold water, a shower, flush toilet, solar lighting, bunks with mattresses, a 2-plate gas stove, a kettle, basic crockery and cutlery, and an outside braai area. Order braai wood from Buffelsfontein Visitor Centre beforehand. PLEASE MAKE SURE YOUR FIRE IS PROPERLY EXTINGUISHED. Don't feed baboons, and pack away all food securely.

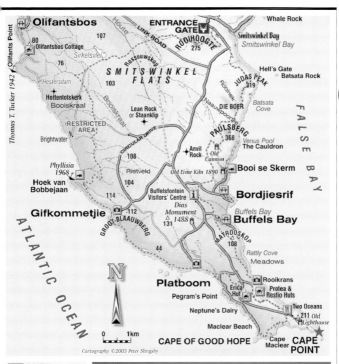

Cartography ©2003 Peter Slingsby

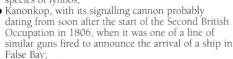

A NEW TRAIL

The five-day, six-night Hoerikwaggo Trail from Cape Town to Cape Point is due to open in late 2004.
℡ (021) 701-8692

lepido-carpodendron) and the Waboom (*P. nitida*); carpets of white everlastings (*Syncarpha vestita*) in summer; and many other species of fynbos;

Vantage point: The rocks at the old signalling cannon on top of Kanonkop give sweeping views to Cape Point.

- Kanonkop, with its signalling cannon probably dating from soon after the start of the Second British Occupation in 1806, when it was one of a line of similar guns fired to announce the arrival of a ship in False Bay;
- the "Knife Edge" walk on Da Gama Peak between the overnight huts and the Cape Point parking area – it sounds scary but it's easy and safe and offers unmatched views;
- the boardwalk from Cape Point to the sheer cliffs of Cape Maclear and the Cape of Good Hope; and
- strolling through the pristine sand dunes at Platboom alongside the rich aquamarine waters of the Atlantic.

MAKING PLANS

The cost of the trail is R80 each for both adults and children (2004 prices). If you have a WILD Card, you will get a 20% discount. No vehicles are allowed at the overnight huts. To book, call the Park's Westlake office, ℡ (021) 701-8692 or the Buffelsfontein Visitor Centre, ℡ (021) 780-9204.

WHAT YOU CAN EXPECT

Distance:
(Clockwise)
Day 1: 10.5km;
Day 2: 19km or 23.3km, depending on whether you include the Cape of Good Hope circuit (recommended)

Time:
Day 1: ±5h;
Day 2: 7h to 9h

Rating: easy walking most of the way

Children: yes, but Day 2 is long and tiring

Dogs: no

Water: carry enough, especially on Day 2

■ A VISIT TO CAPE POINT

In full flight: A Jackal Buzzard at Cape Point.

The wild, wind-swept tip of the Peninsula at Cape Point is one of the most dramatic viewpoints anywhere on Earth, holding each of its 600 000 annual visitors spellbound. Most of them visit this 7 750ha Cape of Good Hope section of the Park for its spectacular landscapes and to savour the romantic, if factually incorrect, atmosphere of the meeting place of the Indian and Atlantic Oceans (▲ 86). But there are many other attractions: like swimming and braaing (barbecuing) at places like Buffels Bay or strolling the many beautiful beaches (▲ 140/1); fishing or diving (▲ 142/3, 144); exploring the shipwrecks (▲ 26/7); watching baboons (▲ 68/9), or just walking through the veld for close-up views of the marvellous flora (▲ 46/51).

Spectacular: The visitor viewing platforms at Cape Point.

A NEW LEASE OF LIFE

WHAT YOU CAN EXPECT

The daily entrance fee (until October 31 2004) is R35 for adults, R10 for scholars, and R10 for pensioners who are South African citizens. WILD Card holders enter free. There is an additional daily fee of R40 per boat, and R20 per individual to carry any marine organisms through the Park, such as fish or rock lobsters (kreef). This section of the Park – still commonly called just 'The Reserve' or 'Cape Point' by many locals – is open from 6am to 6pm from October 1 to March 31, and from 7am to 5pm from April 1 to September 30. Visitors must exit by sunset.

THE KLIPSPRINGER (*Oreotragus oreotragus*) was once widespread on the Peninsula mountain chain, but succumbed to pressures that included frequent fires, hunting – by both humans and feral animals – and competition from the alien Himalayan tahr (▲65). They were locally extinct by the end of the 1930s. In July 1999, a group of 24 were captured in a Boland nature reserve and transferred to the Park where they were released near Olifantsbos in the south. More releases are planned, including on Table Mountain once all the tahrs have been removed.

MARKERS OF THE PAST

Two symbolic *padrãos* have been erected in this section of the Park to honour Portuguese explorers Bartolomeu Dias and Vasco da Gama for their heroic voyages of discovery, and to act as a navigational warning for local sailors. They were designed by sculptor Sydney Hunter, constructed in Salt River and transported to their respective sites in pieces. The Dias *padrão* – painted black on one side to make it more visible against the skyline – stands on a hill close to Buffelsfontein peak; the Da Gama monument is close to Bordjiesrif. When aligned from False Bay, they indicate the direction of submerged Whittle Rock, a major shipping hazard now also marked by a buoy. The *padrãos* were unveiled in 1965 by the Portuguese ambassador. In 1988, another small *padrão* was erected at Buffels Bay to commemorate the quincentenary of Dias's landing.

Majestic: Eland are shy animals and visitors will be lucky to see them.

THE LEGEND OF ADAMASTOR

The story of the mythical monster Adamastor, the grisly Spirit of the Cape of Storms, is told by the great Portuguese poet, Luis Vaz de Camoes, in his epic 16th century poem *Os Lusiadas*. One stanza in his lengthy epic tells that, as the early Portuguese seafarers approached the Cape of Storms, a dark, ominous cloud appeared overhead in the shape of a monstrous human figure and reproached the frightened mariners for venturing into his domain. He prophesied disaster for anyone daring to round the Cape. The monster then revealed himself as Adamastor: in classical mythology, one of the 12 Titans – the children of Uranus (heaven) and Gaea (earth) – who attempted to overthrow the top-ranking gods. But they were defeated and punished by being turned into stone and banished to the furthest corners of the earth – Adamastor to the Cape Point cliffs.

Glorious isolation: the Olifantsbos cottage.

A STYLISH GETAWAY

FOR A 'GETAWAY' IN WILD, unspoiled surroundings less than an hour from Cape Town, spend a few days at Olifantsbos Cottage or at one of two cottages – Duiker and Eland – at Klaasjagersberg. Olifantsbos is the former Skaife Environmental Centre, now converted into a luxuriously appointed, self-catering homestead. It has a master bedroom with a double bed, and two other rooms each with twin beds. There is also an Annex cottage that sleeps six. The modern, fully equipped kitchen has a gas stove and gas fridge, and braai facilities both under cover and outside in a sheltered *lapa* (bush clearing). Lighting is solar-powered.

The cost (2004 prices) is R1 600 per night for the homestead and R150 per person per night in the Annex. The Klaasjagersberg cottages each sleep six and both cost R560 per night.

To book, contact the Park's head office, ✆ (021) 701-8692 or Fax (021) 701-8773, or the Buffelsfontein Visitor Centre ✆ (021) 780-9204 or Fax (021) 780-9321. E-mail: **capepeninsula@parks-sa.co.za** On the Web: **www.cpnp.co.za**

The Flying Dutchman funicular that runs between the main Cape Point parking area and the Old Lighthouse on the summit, replaced the diesel-powered bus of the same name which for many years trundled up and down this track, belching black smoke. The funicular operates from 9.30am each day, and runs every three minutes during peak season. Each car can take a maximum of 40 passengers, and the system can transport a maximum of 450 people per hour. The trip up the 585m track, with its 16 degree incline, takes three minutes. The lower funicular station is 127m above sea level, and the upper station 214m.

The fares (2004 prices) are: Adults R29 return, R20 single; Scholars (under 18) R16 return, R8 single

Birds of a feather: African Penguins are very sociable birds, but also display some odd individual behaviour.

Penguins are among the creatures most loved by people, and with good reason, for they are perhaps the most human of all birds. Slow, comical and clumsy on land, they are incredibly swift and graceful in the water. Brave, loyal to their partners and good socialisers, they are also feisty individuals given to odd eccentricities. Penguins are a flagship species for conservation, and nowhere else on Earth is a member of this remarkable family as accessible to people as at Boulders.

UP CLOSE AND PERSONAL

THE AFRICAN PENGUIN (*Spheniscus demersus*) is one of 17 penguin species, all of which occur in the southern hemisphere. It is Africa's only penguin, with a breeding range from Namibia to Algoa Bay (Port Elizabeth) in the Eastern Cape. There are 27 breeding colonies, 24 on offshore islands where protection from predators is greatest. Mainland breeding colonies are rare because the birds are much more vulnerable here. The first mainland colony was discovered at Sylvia Hill, Namibia in 1980, and the second in November 1982 at Stony Point, Betty's Bay. Then, in 1984, a pair was spotted on a nest at Boulders Beach, a sheltered cove nestling between huge granite boulders near Simon's Town. In March the ➤

Under her wing: A newborn chick peeks out at the world.

I **SCRUFFY SEASON** African Penguins moult once a year – sometimes twice – usually between November and January. During the moult, which lasts 19 or 20 days, they cannot go to sea to feed because they are not waterproof, and they can look incredibly ragged and even ill. But even though a bird may lose almost half its body weight during this period, it is still perfectly healthy, albeit hungry. They must not be disturbed in any way during this time.

I The Boulders penguin colony is one of only four places in the Park where visitors pay an entry fee. In 2004, it was R15 for adults, R5 for scholars and South African pensioners. WILD Card holders enter free. ℂ (021) 786-2329. NOTE: no dogs are permitted on any beaches at Boulders, and they must be on a leash on the coastal path, Willis Walk. CHECK: the tides. Some beaches may be inaccessible.

Perfect viewing: A boardwalk gets visitors close to the birds.

THE SECRET OF WATER FLIGHT

The African Penguin was formerly known as the Jackass Penguin because of its loud, donkey-like braying call. The juvenile birds are entirely blue-grey in colour and lack the adults' 'penguin suit' colouration, white face markings and characteristic black breast band. Penguins breed throughout the year, but the peak is from March to May. They usually produce two eggs which hatch in about 40 days, and the chicks – usually only one survives – take from 60 to 130 days to fledge. African Penguins eat mainly shoaling fish like pilchards and anchovies and also squid. They swim at an average 7km/h, but can reach 20km/h when hunting. Flightless on land, they literally 'fly' through the water, using their hard flippers and steering with their webbed feet. They usually dive less than 30m for about two to five minutes when feeding, but have been recorded at a depth of 130m. Birds of this species usually live for about 10 or 11 years, but a ringed individual was recorded at the ripe old age of 24.

ℹ WHITE GOLD

The pre-colonial era size of the African Penguin population is unknown, but it must have been huge. However, the great guano rush from the early 1840s to harvest the 'white gold' used as fertiliser had a major negative impact on the penguins, which nested in burrows in this guano. At the turn of the 20th century, the population was probably around 2 million, but then it was hit by commercial egg-collecting – between 1900 and 1930, some 13 million eggs were collected on Dassen Island alone. Although egg-collecting was finally stopped in 1968, this period also saw the near-total collapse of pilchard stocks through over-fishing and a switch to targeting anchovies – both important penguin prey items. Oil pollution is another major threat. The total African Penguin population is now estimated at about 179 000 adult birds, including about 56 000 breeding pairs, and it is listed as 'Vulnerable' in the Red Data Book.

Safe cove: Boulders is well protected.

➤ following year these birds laid their first eggs, and the new African Penguin colony was born. Scientists and local residents – not all of whom appreciated the development – have been astounded by the rapid growth of this colony. Since 1985, penguin numbers at Boulders have increased on average by more than 60% each year, and now there are about 3 000 birds here. They are accustomed to human presence and this is the only place in the world where you can get this close to wild penguins – but don't try to touch them! Boardwalks have been constructed to assist visitors, and the best viewing and photography points are at Foxy Beach.

⚠ WARNING

Do not attempt to touch penguins or get too close to them. They have extremely sharp and powerful beaks which can inflict a serious bite – and they are not shy to use them.

Non-swimmers: Youngsters await feeding.

139

■ BEACHES IN THE PARK

A COLONIAL CREATURE

The feared bluebottle, also known as the Portuguese man-o'-war (*Physalia utriculus*), frequently washes up on local beaches. Actually, it is not a single animal, but a colony of animals living permanently attached to one another, each with a highly specialised function. It has a gas-filled float, and its tentacles can be up to 10m long but can contract to just 30cm. The bluebottle inflicts a painful sting, which can be treated with vinegar and ice. Severe stinging is potentially lethal, and should be referred to a doctor immediately.

The Cape Peninsula is blessed with some of the finest beaches in the world, ranging from the four sheltered coves of Clifton where the city's beautiful people gather to tan and strut their stuff on the sparkling white sands, to the family beaches like Fish Hoek where toddlers splash happily in the gentle surf. Most of these highly popular beaches are not in the Park. While a few of the beaches that are in the Park are also popular for recreation – like Buffels Bay and Scarborough – most are still relatively pristine natural areas that are managed for conservation. **Note: swimming anywhere is at your own risk!**

ECOSYSTEMS IN THEIR OWN RIGHT

BEACHES ARE MUCH more than just congenial places to tan and swim – they are also fully functioning ecosystems and habitats for a wide variety of creatures, although species richness on the Park's beaches is much lower than the adjoining rocky shores, mainly because of the reduced diversity of habitat. Beaches are also a harsh environment – alternately covered with water and often subjected to high energy waves, and then totally exposed to the desiccating rays of the sun. Species that occur here have evolved special adaptations that allow them to cope with these conditions.

Solitude: Ratelklip at the northern end of Noordhoek Beach, below Chapman's Peak.

Rainbow colours: Limpets are herbivores and graze on algae.

Merma Pu
Egg cas
the D
Shysh

Platboom: A peaty stream flows over the boulder-strewn beach.

Beach treasure: The colourful remains of a West Coast Rock Lobster

One of the most prolific creatures is the Beach Hopper (*Talorchestia capenis*). During the day it burrows in dry sand or hides under drift material; at night it hops around the beach, feeding on freshly washed up seaweed. Another common species is the Plough Shell (*Bullia* spp), which lives buried low on the beach and surfs up on the waves, using its huge flat foot, to feed on carrion higher up the beach. It is often found in large numbers on stranded bluebottles or jellyfish. The dunes that form at the landward side of the highwater mark support several species of specially adapted plants, and provide nesting sites for a number of coastal birds, such as the endemic African Black Oystercatcher (*Haematopus moquini*) and the White-fronted Plover (*Charadrius marginatus*).

Summer splendour: The sparkling beach at Buffels Bay.

WHERE THEY DARE TO BARE

SANDY BAY, ON THE ATLANTIC SEABOARD is still the only recognised nudist beach on the Peninsula, although it is also visited by non-nudists who enjoy its azure waters and sparkling white sands. Because of its relative isolation, Sandy Bay became popular with nudists in the 1960s. The then highly conservative apartheid government did not approve and there were periodic raids by police, until 1982 when a conviction of public indecency was appealed in the Cape High Court.

Hands off! Nudists on Sandy Bay beach vote to oppose development plans during the 1970s.

In a landmark judgment, Justice Leo van den Heever found that appearing nude on the beach did not *per se* constitute indecent or depraved behaviour. Nudists rejoiced, but Sandy Bay's future was yet not secured. Much of it was actually privately owned, and there were still long and bitter battles with developers who wanted to build houses and a hotel on its pristine shores. Only in the 1990s was its future secured when the then owners, Absa Bank, negotiated an agreement whereby they were allowed to develop a limited number of houses on the eastern (Hout Bay) side of the dunes, in return for donating the remaining 270ha as a nature reserve, later incorporated into the Park.

! SWIMMING: S = Safe; C = Extra care; D = Dangerous

Not all the beaches listed here are in the Park.

Muizenberg S	Platboom C
Danger Beach D	Scarborough D
Fish Hoek S	Witsand C
Glencairn S	Long Beach C
Long Beach	Noordhoek D
(Simon's Town) S	Hout Bay S
Boulders S	Sandy Bay C
Miller's Point S	Llandudno C
Smitswinkel Bay C	Oudekraal C
Buffels Bay C	Camps Bay C
Dias Beach D	Clifton C

TIDAL POOLS:
There are three tidal pools in the Park, all in pay areas: Buffels Bay and Bordjiesrif, both in the Cape of Good Hope section on the False Bay coast, and Oudekraal on the Atlantic Ocean side.

■ Lifesavers are only on duty at some beaches in summer.

BEWARE OF RED TIDES

So-called 'red tides' occur occasionally on the Cape's coasts, and some are potentially dangerous to people who consume affected shellfish such as black and white mussels, clams or oysters during these events. Red tides – they can also be brown, orange, purple or yellow.– are caused by extremely dense concentrations of phytoplankton, the microscopic plants of the sea. Most local red tides, which tend to occur during still periods in late summer or autumn, are caused by a single group of phytoplankton known as dinoflagellates, some of which produce highly potent toxins. Shellfish are vulnerable because they feed by filtering particles from the water, including phytoplankton, and hence accumulate the toxins. If people consume these affected shellfish, they can become very ill or even die. Red tides are closely monitored and appropriate warnings given on a phone Red Tide Hotline. (▲ 180)

■ ANGLING IN THE PARK

Galjoen, South Africa's national fish

When it comes to rock and surf angling, the Table Mountain National Park offers some of the most spectacularly beautiful and infinitely variable fishing places anywhere on the South African coastline. Those who are able to make use of its beaches, gullies, rocky points and ledges are privileged indeed.

Rom abc

Ze

Musselcracker

TIGHT LINES AT EVERY TURN

So WHAT'S THE SECRET to catching the many fish species that abound here? The regulars say: "Leave home earlier and walk further" because the best fishing is going to be at those less popular spots which are not as convenient to reach. But for obvious safety reasons, always try to have at least one companion with you.

One of South Africa's most famous fishing spots is situated in the heart of the Park: the ledges at Rooikrans, just north of Cape Point on the False Bay side. This spot has an awesome reputation for producing huge fish, but be warned: reaching the ledges involves a stiff and potentially hazardous climb down the side of the cliff. And if you happen to have a successful day, the climb back up, carrying all your fishing gear as well

as a couple of Yellowtail or Geelbek, is not for the faint-hearted. But if you're a novice set on a visit to these famous ledges, wait in the car park and before setting out, talk to one of the Rooikrans regulars who can give you advice. Most of the fishing here is done with spinners, and being able to cast a fair distance is a distinct advantage. Yellowtail are also caught at other spots on the False Bay coastline where the steep rock faces end abruptly at deep water or where there is a point of rock reaching out to deeper water. These deep spots are also likely places to find

! **MAKE SURE YOU'RE LEGAL!**
To fish anywhere in South Africa, you require a recreational fishing licence, obtainable at major post offices. The annual licence fee in 2004 was R65. On the same licence form is a "section 9" which covers the collection of most baits for an additional R60. Then the Park also charges R20 per person to carry any marine organism through the Cape of Good Hope pay section of the Park, in addition to the normal entrance fee. National bag limits and marine sanctuary areas are strictly enforced throughout the Park.

WHAT YOU CAN EXPECT

You can expect to catch a large variety of fish from the shoreline of the Park, ranging from Elf, Kob, Geelbek (Cape Salmon – literally, 'yellow mouth') and Yellowtail to Galjoen and White Steenbras, as well as the smaller species like Strepie, Blacktail, Rock Cod and White Stumpnose.

Red Steenbras

Optimistic: Anglers try their luck at Neptune's Dairy on the Park's west coast.

High point: An angler is hardly visible on the cliffs of Cape Maclear.

SUPERB FISHING
BUT TAKE CARE!

To reach the Rooikrans fishing ledges, drive just over 10km from the Cape Point entrance gate to a traffic circle, and turn left up the hill to a parking area; the path down is indicated here.

WARNING: It is not an easy path and is potentially hazardous, especially combined with alcohol. It will take 15 to 30 minutes to get down, and anything from 20 to 45 minutes to get back up, depending on how many fish you're carrying! Don't fish alone, and please take all litter back and help clean any mess left by the less considerate anglers.

the occasional Geelbek.

It seems only fitting that South Africa's national fish, the Galjoen, should have the Park as one of its recognised homes. The fish abounds during winter months when storms and strong seas have washed the gullies clean of sand and exposed the growth on rocks that is the Galjoen's food. Red-bait, which is freely available washed up on beaches, remains the bait of choice for this fish – whether fresh or old and smelly is up to you. White or Black Mussel or Sand Prawn are also used for Galjoen. Look for some white water, the rougher the better: this, on the incoming tide, is where you're likely to find feeding Galjoen. – *Peter Goosen*

◄ CAPE SPECIALS

1 White Stumpnose
2 Blacktail
3 White Steenbras
4 Kob
5 Strepie
6 Yellowtail

USING A BOAT There is a small craft slipway at Buffels Bay in the Cape of Good Hope pay section of the Park. The cost is R40 to take a boat into the Park (2004), whether you launch or not.

Good catch! This Geelbek haul was at the legendary Rooikrans ledges.

143

■ DIVING AND SURFING

Dive time: Divers prepare to enter the sea at Boulders Beach.

Permit required: Mussels can be collected outside the marine reserve – with a permit.

From the top: Multi-coloured Sea fan; Nippled Sea fan; and False plum anemones.

! COLLECTING MUST BE LEGAL

Get your permit to fish or collect marine organisms like rock lobster and mussels from a Post Office. Call ✆ (021) 590-5400 to find out where the nearest Post Office is.

The ocean with its constantly changing moods and appearance is a source of wonder and delight to people all over the world, and the marine component of the Park is no exception. Whether you're a surfer revelling in the awesome power of its waves, a snorkeller floating on its surface and marvelling at the life below, or a diver exploring the extraordinary life of its usually secret depths, the sea off the Park's coastline beckons enticingly.

BLOWING BUBBLES

AS WITH SO MANY other activities, the Peninsula is extremely highly rated when it comes to diving, because of the different habitats associated with the different marine provinces (▲ 86/7), and because its two coastlines react so differently to the weather conditions. So when a south-easterly wind is howling in summer, it's quite likely that there will be great – but cold! – diving conditions at Oudekraal on the Atlantic, while winter's stormy north-westers often

Divers' delights: Root-mouthed Jellyfish, above, and the Cowled Nudibranch.

make for ideal diving in False Bay. The Atlantic Ocean is coldest, with temperatures as low as 10 Deg C because of upwelling, and particularly in summer when conditions are best. This coast offers some spectacular wreck dives, and the kelp forests are a speciality. In False Bay, the water will be 12 to 18 Deg C in winter when the sea is flattest and cleanest. A special attraction here are the five wrecks scuttled by the SA Navy off Smitswinkel Bay in the 1970s to create an artificial reef. On the Web: www.Cybercapetown.com/DiveCapeTown/

Pumping: A big swell in False Bay makes a great break at Black Rocks near Bordjiesrif.

TUBES, BARRELS AND BREAKS

THE CAPE PENINSULA OFFERS the greatest concentration and variety of surfing spots in South Africa, with at least 50 within one hour's drive of the city centre. Some of these are still jealously guarded by those in the know, but it's an unusual day when you can't find at least one popular spot that's working well, although it may be pretty crowded as a result. Most of the breaks are on the Atlantic or western side of the Peninsula, where the water can be seriously cold and wetsuits are a prerequisite. False Bay is much warmer.

Top-rated local surf spots include:
• *The Hoek*, at the foot of Chapman's Peak;
• *Dunes*, mid-way along Noordhoek Beach;
• *Outer Kom*, near Slangkop lighthouse;
• *365*, further south than the Kom;
• *Crayfish Factory*, at the far end of Witsand;
• *Olifantsbos*, in the Cape Point pay section;
• *Buffels Bay* and *Black Rocks*, also in this pay section. Both spots need a big swell to work well.

Working the waves: Surfers show their classic styles at Long Beach.

On the Web: www.wavescape.co.za/top_bar/spots/capetown.html

ℹ SURFERS IN THE KNOW
• Daily Surf Report ✆ 082 234-6370.
• The Weather Office ✆ 082 162 issues daily tide and wind reports.
• On the Web: www.wpsurfing. co.za
• Waveski surfing: www.geocities. com/Colosseum/ Stadium/5746/

Ocean delights: A licensed diver with his catch of perlemoen at Buffels Bay. In the 2003/4 season recreational catches of perlemoen were banned.

Rock life: A Spiny Starfish, above; and a Reticulated Starfish and a Red Starfish, below.

■ CLIMBING AND CAVING

Several steps up: A climber on the famous Jacob's Ladder on Table Mountain.

THE CHALLENGE OF HIGH PLACES

BY THE EARLY 1890s, several rock climbing routes were being opened on Table Mountain – all without safety equipment like ropes and belays. The first famous local "name" was Jim Searle, and the sport developed very rapidly after 1895, especially with the achievements of first George Travers-Jackson and later others like Bert Berrisford, George Londt, Joe Marcus, Ken Cameron, Mike Mamacos, Barry Fletcher and Michael Scott. Now, more than 640 routes have been opened.

Until the 1980s, climbers had little impact on the mountain, other than some trampling in popular areas or occasional littering. But through the 1980s, and starting on Lion's Head, fixed protection in the form of permanent bolts began to make an appearance. Termed "sport climbing", this new development in safety led to a huge increase in the popularity of climbing – but with it came increased environmental degradation, particularly with the wholesale placing of bolts on rock faces. Following intensive discussions between the local climbing fraternity and Park management, any proposed new sport route must now be approved by a joint Sport Climbing Working Committee. Also, an Environmental Policy for Climbing has been developed which all climbers using the Park are expected to adhere to.

A LEGEND IN HIS OWN LIFETIME
Climbing prodigy George Travers-Jackson was accepted into the Mountain Club of SA aged just 14 in 1894, and was Secretary from 1899-1910. In just 12 years – 1895 to 1907 – he took part in 51 first ascents on Table Mountain, one of which was of G-grading, climbed without safety equipment.

HEADING FOR THE DARKNESS

The Peninsula mountain chain has some of the largest sandstone cave systems in the world, one of which is in the Back Table area. Here, well-known Wynberg Cave was visited regularly as long ago as the 1890s. However, it was only in the 1950s that exploration of this extensive cave system started, initiated by well-known author and mountaineer Jose

With care: A well-equipped caver worms his way through a passage in one of Kalk Bay mountain's many caves.

Burman. The other big cave system in the Park is in the Kalk Bay mountains, which was explored and mapped in the 1930s by a group of young enthusiasts under the leadership of retired teacher Johan Meyer, who dubbed his group 'The Moles'. By 1941, they had discovered some 60 caves here, and were responsible for some of the nicknames in this area which still persist – like 'Wandering Willy's Weary Wait'. (▲ 126/7) Today, more than 100 caves are known in this area.

■ Serious cavers who want to join the Cape Peninsula Speleological Society can call ✆ (021) 696-0196, after hours, or email **capesec@telkomsa.net**
WARNING: All the caves on the mountain, even popular ones like Boomslang, are either potentially dangerous or extremely hazardous, and people without proper experience and/or a knowledgeable guide should not enter any cave. The Cave Peak area of Kalk Bay is especially dangerous, with hidden drops of up to 15m.

ENVIRONMENTAL POLICY FOR CLIMBING

IN TERMS OF A NEGOTIATED ENVIRONMENTAL POLICY, climbers using the Park's many fully equipped sport climbing routes have agreed to minimise the negative aspects and to promote the safe practice of their sport. In terms of this policy, they are committed to:

● Minimising the impact of climbing activities on the natural environment of the Park, including all indigenous fauna and flora;
● Minimising the visual impact of fixed protection;
● Minimising impacts on the cultural and historical environment, including archaeological and palaeontological sites;
● Adhering to standards for fixed protection that conform to appropriate safety standards;
● Identifying and assessing the significance of impacts associated with potential new climbing areas in conjunction with SA National Parks and other climbers;
● Co-operating with the Park's management and recognising and responding to their concerns; and
● Monitoring sport-climbing activities to ensure compliance with the above principles.
On the Web: **www.cpnp.co.za**

🛈 GETTING THERE
There are a number of commercial operators who will take visitors on climbs on Table Mountain of various grades, depending on their experience. Contact Cape Town Tourism for details (▲ 180). Visitors can also contact the Cape Town section of the Mountain Club of South Africa, at 97 Hatfield Street, Cape Town 8001. ✆ (021) 465-3412 Fax (021) 461-8456 e-mail: **mcsacapetown@iafrica.com** On the Web: **http://cap.mcsa.org.za**

■ CYCLING AND RUNNING

Scenic splendour
Competitors in the Cape
Argus Cycle Tour pedal
towards Smitswinkel Bay
with Judas Peak looming
in the background

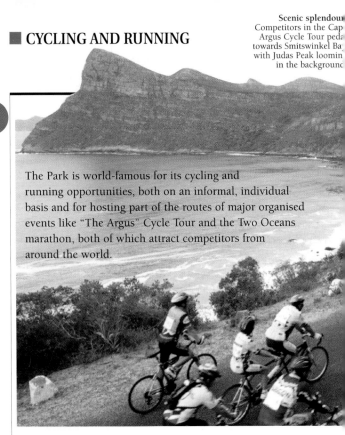

The Park is world-famous for its cycling and running opportunities, both on an informal, individual basis and for hosting part of the routes of major organised events like "The Argus" Cycle Tour and the Two Oceans marathon, both of which attract competitors from around the world.

JOIN IN THE FUN
The Cape Argus/ Pick 'n Pay Cycle Tour is the largest timed cycling event in the world, with some 35 000 entrants. A significant part of its 109km circular route around the Peninsula is through the Park. Riders come from all over the world to take part in 'The Argus', as its commonly known. The race is so popular that entries open in September and are usually filled within days.
On the Web: **www.cycletour. co.za**

MORE THAN JUST A WALK

FOR THOSE WHO LIKE TO GO FASTER than just walking pace, the Park offers an enormous variety of cycling and running routes, both on- and off-road. These include several official races which are held entirely or partly in the Park, and which all attract large fields – partly because of the superb scenery en route. One of the most popular cycling areas is the Cape of Good Hope section, from the main gate down to Cape Point. You don't even need your own bicycle – commercial operators will provide the necessary. For information: Cape Town Tourism (▲ 180). On the Web: **www.pedalpower.co.za**

FROM ONE OCEAN TO ANOTHER

The Two Oceans Marathon, a 56km ultra-marathon that takes in views of both the Indian and Atlantic Oceans, is one of the world's most scenic road races and, after Comrades, probably South Africa's most popular long run. The route goes through part of the Park: prior to 2000, and again from 2004 onwards, it includes the famous Chapman's Peak Drive. On the Web: **www. twooceansmarathon. org.za**

THE PARK'S OWN ROAD RACE

The inaugural Cape Point Half Marathon was in 2002, when 1048 athletes ran the standard 21.1km route between the Klaasjagersbos office and Buffels Bay. From 2003, a slightly different route was used, starting near, and finishing at, Buffels Bay. This race, run annually in January, is organised by the Gugulethu Athletics Club, assisted by the Park, and is held under the auspices of Athletics South Africa and Western Province Athletics and Road Running. On the Web: **www.wpa.org.za**

RUNNING WITH NATURE

FEW OTHER CITIES IN THE WORLD offer such unrivalled off-road running opportunities – most of them virtually on runners' doorsteps. One of the best known off-road runs is the "Puffer" – technically, the 80km Peninsula Ultra Marathon – run mostly off-road from Cape Point to the V&A Waterfront

Off-road: Runners on Devil's Peak.

through the Park. It is organised by the Fish Hoek Athletics Club and entries are strictly limited. Visit **www.puffer.co.za** and see also **www.crag.org.za**

Tough but scenic: The 'Puffer' Ultra Marathon.

■ ADVENTURE SPORTS

Hang over the edge of a sheer 100-metre cliff and shiver at the sight of the sea pounding below. Soar in quiet solitude along the ridge of the Twelve Apostles in a paraglider, or stop paddling your sea kayak to admire the porpoising of African Penguins as they race past you in False Bay.

Like a bird: Paragliding from Lion's Head, one of two Park-approved launch sites. To fly, ✆ (021) 438-1512 (o/h). The other site is in Silvermine: ✆ (021) 701-8692.

Concentrate fiercely as you fly down a rough gravel track on the mountain's lower slopes on your bike. If you're looking for adventures like these, the Park offers a host of opportunities.

ADRENALIN JUNKIES IN THE PARK

ROCK-CLIMBING, ABSEILING, single or tandem paragliding, hiking and mountain walking, surfing, wind-surfing, kite-surfing, mountain biking, sea kayaking, orienteering, reef diving, wreck diving, deep sea spearfishing, snorkelling, sailing, game fishing, high-speed boat riding, shark cage-diving, caving, mountain running and horse riding ... the range of sport opportunities in and around the Park is enormous.

Brave hearts: A surfer wipes out during the Big Wave contest at Dungeons, above, and paddleskiers battle it out – both off the Sentinel at Hout Bay.

The Park does not itself organise or in any way officially sponsor or endorse any of the many adventure sports which take place within its boundaries, and anyone taking part in such activities does so entirely at his or her own risk.

However, there are many commercial operators who offer very exciting but safe activities in a wide range of adventure sports.

To find out what's on offer, visit one of Cape Town Tourism's many outlets – for full contact details, ▲ 180.

Going with flow: A kite surfer does his thing at Witsand beach, between Kommetjie and Scarborough.

PEDALLING PAST PROBLEMS

The Park has the potential to be a world-class mountain biking venue, but in 2004 there were still very few areas open for this sport. The main mountain bike area is Tokai Forest which in 2004 was still outside the Park, managed by MTO Forestry. A major long-term goal is the development of a mountain biking route from Signal Hill to Simon's Town and, if possible, all the way to Cape Point, but in 2004 that was still way off. There is wide recognition that mountain bikes (MTBs) can impact negatively on both the environment – through trail erosion and compaction – and on other users, unless managed properly. An Environmental Management Policy for biking in the Park has been developed by the MTB committee of the Pedal Power Association, ✆ (021) 689-8420 in collaboration with Park management. Bikers should familiarise themselves with this policy and with the areas where mountain biking is currently allowed in the Park. On the Web: **www.cpnp.co.za** and **www.pedalpower.co.za**

> **!** In the Silvermine area of the Park, biking is allowed on designated trails in the northern section only; there is no biking on the southern (Muizenberg) side.

Blur of speed: A competitor in a mountain bike race flies down the track on the mountain's slopes.

Go for it! Mountain biking on the lower slopes of Table Mountain, and abseiling at Chapman's Peak.

151

RESTAURANTS, BRAAIS AND PICNICS

Park visitors have plenty of choices about where to eat. There's the luxury and comfort of being indoors at facilities carefully situated in some of the Park's most spectacular settings; alternatively, enjoy the traditional South African lifestyle and savour the special pleasure of doing your own cooking outdoors over a "braai" fire.

INDOOR OR OUTDOOR INDULGENCE

IN KEEPING WITH THE PARK'S ROLE as custodian of one of the world's biodiversity "hot-spots" and of spectacular natural scenery, built infrastructure within its boundaries is being kept to a minimum and any new developments restricted to existing "footprints". The only major structures are those the Park inherited: Table Mountain's cableway complex and the restaurant/funicular at Cape Point, both managed by concessionaires and both offering excellent dining. Other Park facilities are low-key, with an emphasis on outdoor, family-oriented recreational activity.

Choices: The Cape Point restaurant's spectacular views over False Bay, above, and the popular Buffels Bay tidal pool and picnic/braai complex, left.

Top grilling: The popular braai sites at Silvermine reservoir were relandscaped after the wildfires in 2000.

WHERE TO PICNIC AND BRAAI (BARBECUE)
(maps ▲170/75)

Picnics only:
Signal Hill
The Glen
Van Riebeeck Park
Constantia Nek

Picnics and braais:
Newlands Forest
Oudekraal
Silvermine
Bordjiesrif
Buffels Bay
Schusterskraal
  (Scarborough)
Perdekloof/
Wildschutsbrand

Outside the Park:
Kirstenbosch (picnic only)
Chapman's Peak
  (picnic only)
Tokai (picnic, braai)
Miller's Point (picnic, braai)
Soetwater (picnic, braai)
Zandvlei (picnic, braai) (Muizenberg)

WHERE CHEFS DO THE WORK

Cape Point:
Two Oceans
Restaurant
© (021)780-9200

Table Mountain,
Bistro, restaurant at the Upper Cable Station
© (021)424-8181

Rhodes Memorial:
Tea garden and curio shop
© (021) 689-9151

Kirstenbosch:
Various options
© (021)762-9585

Tokai Arboretum:
Tea garden
© (021)715-4512

THE TOKAI ARBORETUM

Commercial forestry on Table Mountain started when Paul Schiekerdanz was appointed forest guard and ranger in 1884. One year later, the Conservator of Forests of the then Western Conservancy of the Cape Colony, Joseph Storr Lister, started an arboretum at Tokai to see which exotic tree species would thrive. He planted more than 150 species, including 33 varieties of gum and 20 of pine. This was the foundation of South Africa's forestry industry. The arboretum became a National Monument in 1985. It is not (2004) in the Park.

Snack time: Hikers refuel during a stop near Breakfast Rock on the Smuts Track.

SILVERMINE

This section of the Park was proclaimed as a nature reserve by the City of Cape Town in 1965. It is a very popular picnic and braai (barbecue) area, and is one of four pay entry points. R10 for adults, R5 for children (up to October 31 2004). Gates open at 7am in summer, and at 8am in winter.

153

■ A surfing photographer at The Dungeons (▲145).

■ A perfect evening on the beach at Olifantsbos (▲136/7).

■ From left, Paulsberg, Die Boer and Judas Peak at dawn (▲134)
154

BEYOND THE PARK
MAPS & CONTACTS

HOW TO FIND WHAT YOU'RE LOOKING FOR AND HOW TO GET WHERE YOU'RE GOING

(AND A FEW OTHER NATIONAL PARKS TO VISIT)

■ A Watsonia at Silvermine (▲120).

■ KIRSTENBOSCH

Common or garden: A Garden Acraea (*Acraea horta*), a common butterfly across the Peninsula.

Kirstenbosch National Botanical Garden is not part of the Park, although the upper part of this estate – starting from the Contour Path (▲110/15) – is managed by the Park for the responsible authority, the National Botanical Institute. But a visit to this world-famous garden, and particularly any extended visit which includes a walk into the forest area or along the mountainside, is an intimate part of the overall visitor experience of the Park.

Disa atricapilla

Standing proud: Tree Ferns in the garden.

A LONG AND FASCINATING HISTORY

Mandela's Gold: A specially bred *Strelitzia* named for ex-president Nelson Mandela.

KIRSTENBOSCH COVERS AN AREA of 532 hectares of which 36 ha is cultivated. The estate's recorded history starts in October 1657 when Leendert Cornelissen of Zevenhuysen was granted the right to work the forests on the eastern slopes of Table Mountain as a *vrijtimmerman* (free carpenter) and woodcutter. This area became known as Leendertsbos, and when and why it later became Kirstenbosch is not known. However, speculation is that it may have been named after Dutch East India Company official Johann Kirsten. Around 1760, Company woodcutters previously based at Paradijsbos (Newlands Forest) moved south to work at a buitepos (outpost) then already known as Kirstenbosch.

Often seen: The Small Grey Mongoose is a common resident.

I GETTING THERE
Situated in Newlands off the M63, Rhodes Drive, the garden is open every day of the year, from 8am to 7pm in summer and 8am to 6pm in winter.
✆(021)799-8899
Fax (021)797-6570.
E-mail:
kirstenboschinfo @nbict.nbi.ac.za
For information on the National Botanical Institute
✆(021)799-8800.
On the Web:
www.nbi.ac.za
Members of the Botanical Society
✆(021)797-2090
have free entry to all national botanical gardens in South Africa.

Spectacular blooms: *Leucospermum oleifolium*, above, and a pincushion, *Leucospermum* sp, below.

Quiet space: Many visit for the tranquillity of the gardens.

Lovely beyond words: Kirstenbosch's world-famous setting below Table Mountain.

During the British Occupations (1795-1803, and 1806 onwards), Kirstenbosch became government property. In 1811, it was divided into two freehold land grants. The upper portion went to Colonel Christopher Bird, Deputy Colonial Secretary, who constructed the outdoor "bird" bath still in existence today in the Dell – often incorrectly associated with Lady Anne Barnard. The lower portion went to Colonial Secretary Henry Alexander. Bird soon sold his property for £1 000 to Alexander. Later, from 1823, it was owned by the Eksteen and then the Cloete families, and from the mid-19th century many fruit trees and oaks were planted. Rhodes acquired the Kirstenbosch estate in December 1895 for £9 000, and left it to the people of South Africa on his death in 1902 (▲ 32/3).

Kirstenbosch was declared a National Botanical Garden in 1913, and the first curator was Dr Harold Pearson.

I LIFE'S A HOOT: The Spotted Eagle-Owl (*Bubo africanus*) breeds regularly in the Camphor Avenue in Kirstenbosch, where its chicks (above) peer down at visitors making their way to the highly popular Summer Sunset Concert series.

Feature: Zimbabwean soapstone sculptures grace Kirstenbosch.

A WEALTH OF THINGS TO DO

Acclaimed as one of the world top seven botanical gardens and arguably the best in the southern hemisphere, Kirstenbosch offers many attractions. Apart from a huge plant collection showcasing South Africa's unique and diverse floral wealth, special attractions include numerous paths through the gardens and several formal trails; a large fynbos garden featuring restios, proteas and ericas; a comprehensive collection of succulents in the Glass Conservatory; a collection of cycads – fascinating plants with an ancient lineage; and a MyGuide electronic self-guiding system. It is also a birder's paradise, with more than 200 species having been recorded.

Beware: A Green-headed Blister Beetle on an iris.

■ RONDEVLEI NATURE RESERVE

NATURAL JEWEL ON THE CITY'S DOORSTEP

ⓘ MAKING CONTACT

✆ (021) 706-2404
Fax: (021) 706-2405
email: **rondevlei@
sybaweb.co.za**
On the Web: **www.
rondevlei.co.za**
Imvubu Nature
Tours
✆ (021) 706-0842
Cell: 072 419-8261
e-mail: **info@
imvubu.co.za**
On the Web: **www.
imvubu.co.za**

RONDEVLEI NATURE RESERVE, managed by the City of Cape Town, is rightly billed as one of the ecological gems of the Cape Flats. Originally established as a bird sanctuary in 1952, it was upgraded to full nature reserve status in 1988. Not only is it a birder's paradise – some 230 species have been recorded here, and there is excellent viewing from six hides – but it helps conserve two of the Cape Floristic Region's most threatened vegetation types: Sand Plain Fynbos and Strandveld. Of the former, 89% has already been lost in the metropolitan area and less than 1% is formally conserved; for the latter, the figures are 58% and less than 10% respectively. It is therefore an extremely important habitat for some very rare plants.

Great White Pelicans

These include the *Serruria foeniculacea*, long thought to have been extinct on the Cape Flats but rescued from a building site just outside the reserve in 1988 by then warden Howard Langley and re-planted in Rondevlei where it now thrives.

Like its neighbour Zeekoevlei, Rondevlei is what is technically known as a shallow lacustrine wetland. A

■ WOLFGAT NATURE RESERVE

WOLFGAT NATURE RESERVE is also managed by the City of Cape Town. It is a stunningly beautiful location, covering some 248ha on the western shores of the False Bay coastline. The heart of Wolfgat, and one of the main reasons for its proclamation, is a one kilometre stretch of calcrete cliff-top which is the only breeding site of the Kelp Gull (*Larus dominicanus*), on the Peninsula. Various raptor species will also be seen here, including the charismatic Peregrine Falcon (*Falco peregrinus*). However, Wolfgat is also significant for its extremely rare Strandveld and Limestone Fynbos vegetation, and the reserve is one of 15 core conservation sites identified by the Botanical Society of SA as essential to be maintained if more than 80% of the Red Data Book plant species on the Cape Flats are to be saved – that is, at least 40 of the 48 endangered plants.

Peregrine Falcon

The management of Wolfgat is beset with problems, partly because it is bisected by the main False Bay coastal road; and also because of the dense urban development on its western borders; a heavy invasion by alien plants; and a lack of management resources.

There are no visitor facilities here, but it is one of the most photogenic places on the Peninsula and well worth a visit. **However, please heed the warning at right!**

Kelp Gull

linking corridor between the two has been acquired for conservation purposes, and the two are also connected via groundwater. Neither vlei (an Afrikaans word for wetland) is now a totally naturally functioning wetland system, because for many decades each has been used as a depository for an increasing volume of stormwater run-off from adjoining urban developments in a 100 sq km catchment. This stormwater is both polluted and, more significantly, loaded with nutrients like phosphorus. Also, the hydraulic systems of both vleis are artificially controlled to a degree by weirs constructed in the 1940s. However, Rondevlei in particular has been rehabilitated very significantly.

Top billing: Hippo were reintroduced to Rondevlei to help control an alien grass.

Birds seen here include the Great White Pelican (*Pelecanus onocrotalus*), Greater Flamingo (*Phoenicopterus ruber*), African Spoonbill (*Platalea alba*), Caspian Tern (*Sterna caspia*) and Grey Heron (*Ardea cinerea*). Mammals include the Cape Clawless Otter (*Aonyx capensis*), Grysbok (*Raphicerus melanotis*), Porcupine (*Hystrix africaeaustralis*), and, of course, the reserve's famous hippo (*Hippopotamus amphibius*).

Rondevlei and other wetland areas on the Cape Flats were historically populated by hippos (▲ 66) but these animals were quickly hunted to local extinction by the early European settlers. To help control an invasive South American grass (*Paspalum* sp), that threatened to overrun the vlei, two male hippos – named Bruno and Brutus – were brought from KwaZulu-Natal in 1981. Later, two females (Cleo and Portia) were introduced to establish a breeding population. The hippos effectively eliminated the *Paspalum* and now play an important ecological role by helping control the growth and spread of bulrushes (*Typha capensis*), and by spreading nutrients through the system via their dung. In early 2004, there were six hippos at Rondevlei.

⚠ WARNING
Wolfgat is isolated, so take particular care when visiting here. Always travel in a group – don't go on your own. Don't leave any valuables in the vehicle and make sure it is properly secured with an anti-theft device. Always carry a cellphone with you.

WEST COAST NATIONAL PARK

Cape Gannet

Spring flowers so vivid you almost need to wear sunglasses to look at them; a languid turquoise lagoon and associated wetlands that constitute one of the world's most important habitats for migratory wading birds; seabirds by the tens of thousands; thunderous waves rolling in from the icy Atlantic and crashing onto white sands; cultural artefacts from our earliest "modern" ancestors – these are just some of the unique mix in the West Coast National Park.

A WORLD FROM ANOTHER ERA

LESS THAN 100KM FROM CAPE TOWN, the West Coast National Park has as its focal point the beautiful Langebaan Lagoon. Long a popular recreational resource for people, the lagoon is equally popular with migrant birds – so popular, in fact, and hence ecologically important, that it is a Ramsar Site (deemed to be of international importance for the conservation of wetland birds). There are also several islands in the lagoon, some of which are major breeding sites for seabirds like the Cape Gannet, Kelp Gull and Hartlaub's Gull.

To satisfy conflicting user demands, the lagoon is divided into three zones: a multi-functional area for all users; a quiet zone for sailing, swimming and canoeing only; and a wilderness area that is closed to the public.

The land section of the park is a conventional reserve which protects Strandveld vegetation and its many associated birds and animals – especially tortoises. Park accommodation is limited, but includes a six-bed houseboat. There are many private establishments near by.

EVE'S FOOTPRINTS
Probably the Park's most important cultural artefact is a trail of fossilised footprints, found in sand dune that had turned to rock and dated at 117 000 years – the oldest known footprints of an anatomically modern human being. Because most scientists believe modern humans evolved in Africa around this time, the find was dubbed 'Eve's footprints'. Because they were extremely vulnerable to erosion in the position where they were found in 1996 – very close to the lagoon edge – they were removed for temporary safekeeping to the Iziko-South African Museum. A cast has been made and the originals will be returned when a suitable repository has been created.

Lagoon look-out: Granite outcrops are a feature of the park's Postberg section.

SPRING SPECIALS:
The Postberg section is privately owned, but is managed by the park on a contractual basis and is open to the public for about two months each spring when the spectacular wildflower displays are in full bloom.

Inquiries:
℡ (022)772-2144
On the Web:
www.parks-sa. co.za/parks/ Westcoast/ default.html

Spring glory: The Postberg section of the Park is famous for its wildflower displays.

Bird habitat: The salt marshes at the southern end of the lagoon are a wader's delight.

THIS PARK HAS BECOME A LEGENDARY BIRDING SITE, best known for the large numbers of migrant waders that crowd the mudflats during summer. The Geelbek mudflat bird hide offers superb wader watching in summer; it is arguably South Africa's best waterbird hide, and the array of desirable vagrant waders found here render it the favoured haunt of dedicated twitchers. It allows for close-up views of a large diversity of wading species; common summer migrants include Curlew Sandpiper, Little Stint, Sanderling, Red Knot, Ruddy Turnstone, Common Greenshank, Marsh Sandpiper (unusually common here), Common Whimbrel, Grey Plover, Common Ringed Plover, Bar-tailed Godwit, and a smaller number of resident White-

Azure waters: Langebaan Lagoon

fronted and Chestnut-banded Plovers. A few of the localised Eurasian Curlew are always present. It usually takes some careful scanning to pick up the scarce but regular Terek Sandpiper and, with luck, Greater Sand Plover or Common Redshank. Timing is very important: this area is at its most rewarding for birders about 4½ hours after high tide in Table Bay. – *Callan Cohen*

Summer visitors: Ruddy Turnstone, above, and Sanderlings are among this park's many Palearctic migrants.

Curlew Sandpiper

■ AGULHAS NATIONAL PARK

Proof: The plaque at the very tip.

THE SOUTHERN-MOST POINT

Cape Agulhas lies at 34 Deg 49' 58" South, 20 Deg 00' 12" East at the very tip of the African continent, and the position is marked by a stone cairn. It is some 230km by road from Cape Town, and is accessed from the N2 highway, turning right at Caledon and driving south via Bredasdorp. The nearest towns are L'Agulhas and the fishing village of Struisbaai. The park is still under development and in early 2004 there were no overnight facilities here yet.
Inquiries:
℃ (028) 435-6222
On the Web:
www.parks-sa.co.za/parks/Agulhas/default.html

Landmark: The famous Agulhas lighthouse, above left, stands close to the rocky spit, above right, at the end of the continent.

THE VERY TIP OF AFRICA

Wrecked: This coastline has claimed numerous victims.

Not even its most ardent supporters will claim that Cape Agulhas is as dramatic as Cape Point, but it's one of those places you simply must visit to be able to say: "I've stood at the very edge of Africa where the Atlantic and Indian Oceans meet." (▲86) It has an atmosphere and special charm of its own, and a first visit is unlikely to be the last.

■ BONTEBOK NATIONAL PARK

LIKE THE UNFORTUNATE BLUE BUCK before it, the Bontebok (*Damaliscus dorcas dorcas*) was well on the way to extinction, with only 17 animals left when the Bontebok National Park was proclaimed in 1931 to help save it. In fact, the Bontebok is closely related to the Blesbok (*D. dorcas phillipsi*): both are sub-species of an antelope (*D. dorcas*) which occurred widely in southern Africa at one time but which then split into two discrete populations – scientists believe this may have been as a result of climate change. In recent times, the Bontebok has been restricted to the fynbos region of the south-western Cape, where it is still endangered. The maximum number that this 2 786ha national park can support is around 200, and over the years its surplus animals have been transferred to sanctuaries, parks and reserves elsewhere in the region. The total population of the Bontebok is now somewhere between 2 000 and 3 000. These antelope are not the only attractions here: there are other mammals and a rich birdlife, as well as the Breede River which flows through

Southern Black Korhaan

Southern-most stroll: The path from the lighthouse to the point.

THE VAST, WIND-SWEPT AGULHAS coastal plain at the southern end of Africa is rich in history and culture, as well as being the habitat of an extremely diverse plant life that, proportionate to size, equals the species richness of the tropical rain forests. Some 2 000 indigenous plants occur here, of which 100 are endemic and at least 110 feature in the Red Data Book. It is therefore an extremely important

Often seen: Common Tern *(Sterna hirundo)*

component of the Cape Floral Kingdom (▲46/51). The Agulhas Plain also has many wetland habitats, with a correspondingly high number of wetland plants, aquatic invertebrates – including the endangered Cape Platanna (▲60) and Micro Frog – and many water birds, both residents and migrants. Cultural artefacts include ancient stone tidal fish

Back from the brink: Bontebok and their light-coloured calves.

the park and offers angling and safe bathing. There are caravan and camping sites close to the river, and fixed accommodation is in the form of six-berth "chalavans".

I **GETTING THERE**
The Bontebok National Park is 6km from the historic town of Swellendam, and lies between the N2 highway and the Breede River. It is 240km from Cape Town and 540km from Port Elizabeth.

INFORMATION:
(028) 514-2735
On the Web:
www.parks-sa. co.za/parks/ Bontebok/ default.html

■ KAROO NATIONAL PARK

Fynbos is South Africa's true ecological gem; the savanna bushveld with its "Big Five" is a tourist favourite; but the Great Karoo is, arguably, the heart of this country. With its vast plains stretching out towards the horizon, characteristic Karoo "koppies" – small, flat-topped hills – and the Nuweveld mountain range with its imposing red dolorite cliffs looming in the background, this Park is a must for visitors and locals.

Park special: Cape Mountain Zebra (*Equus zebra zebra*) foal.

i WHERE AND HOW

The Karoo National Park is situated to the west of Beaufort West, about 500km north of Cape Town, and its entrance is off the N1 highway, just south of the town. It was proclaimed in 1979, but had its origins in a campaign started in the late 1950s by William Quinton, a local farmer and keen birder. The Beaufort West town council donated 7 209ha of communal land as the nucleus of the new park, and since then it has grown substantially. The present size of the park is about 80 000ha.

Home again: One of the Black Rhinos which were reintroduced to the park. This species occurred here historically.

A PLACE TO REFRESH THE SOUL

THE KAROO IS THE LARGEST ECOSYSTEM in the country, and home to a fascinating diversity of life that thrives in what is mostly a harsh environment. The park is particularly diverse because of its elevation range: from 800m, where rainfall is also very low, (175mm) to 1 800m with a relatively high rainfall (406mm). The vegetation includes montane grassland, typical Karoo shrublands and a wide variety of succulent plants. Mammals include Eland, Red Hartebeest, Black Wildebeest, Black Rhino, Springbok and Kudu. There are two zebra species: the endangered Cape Mountain Zebra and the Plains Zebra; the latter are part of the Quagga Project (▲ 33) of which the park is a key partner. The park has a very rich reptilian fauna, including five species of tortoise and 18 different snakes. More than 200 bird species have been recorded, including some 20 pairs of Verreaux's Eagle (Black Eagle) – an exceptional concentration. Facilities include Cape Dutch style cottages and chalets, and camping and caravan sites.

Graceful: Springbok (*Antidorcus marsupialis*), above and below, are the definitive animal of the Great Karoo, historically occurring in herds numbering hundreds of thousands.

Common: The Scrub Hare (*Lepus saxatilis*) is widespread.

■ Contact details: ✆ **(023) 415-2828, fax (023) 415-1671.** On the Web: **www.parks-sa.co.za/parks/Karoo/default.html**

Gentle on the eye: The typical Karoo landscape of the park.

ℹ PARK SPECIALS

The Great Karoo is a particularly rich area for fossils, and the park's 400m Karoo Fossil Braille Trail, specially designed for handicapped visitors, depicts the area's fascinating geology and palaeontology. The park is also a birder's delight, with easy access to three tricky rock-loving species, namely Cinnamon-breasted Warbler, African Rock Pipit and Short-toed Rock-Thrush.

Spike-heeled Lark
(*Chersomanes albofasciata*)

Mountain Wheatear, African Red-eyed Bulbul and Cape Bunting are tame and conspicuous at the Park's headquarters and rest camp, and Verreaux's Eagle regularly passes overhead. Take an amble around the nearby campsite, set in dense acacia thicket, as it offers some of the best birding in the park. Namaqua Warbler, Southern Tchagra, Acacia Pied Barbet, Cardinal Woodpecker, Dusky Sunbird, Pririt Batis, Chestnut-vented Tit-Babbler and Fairy Flycatcher are all vocal but inconspicuous thicket dwellers. Rather more obvious are all three South African mousebird species. Klipspringer Pass drive, which winds up the escarpment of the plateau behind the rest camp, provides access to the three specials of rocky country. Check the slopes at the base of the pass for Layard's Tit-Babbler, African Rock Pipit and Short-toed Rock-Thrush. The vicinity of the fenced lookout point at the summit of the pass is a good site for both Cinnamon-breasted Warbler and African Rock Pipit, neither of which is likely to be seen without staying very alert to their calls. Other mountain species that are typical of the cliffs along the Klipspringer Pass are Verreaux's and Booted Eagle, Ground Woodpecker and Pale-winged Starling. – *Callan Cohen*

Double-banded Courser
(*Rhinoptilus africanus*)

Karoo Korhaan
(*Eupodotis vigorsii*)

Rest camp: Two of the park's cottages, built in a vernacular Cape Dutch style.

Challenging: The rugged 4x4 route tests drivers and vehicles.

165

■ Cape Point surrounded by ocean. (▲22)

■ Wildevoëlvlei outlet at Kommetjie beach. (▲128)

■ Sunset at the Sentinel, Hout Bay. (▲30)

■ Dawn on Paulsberg with a view to Cape Point. (▲134)

■ Early morning: the cannon at King's Blockhouse. (▲110)

■ Cape Fox cubs at Kirstenbosch. (▲156)

MAIN ROUTES
TO
CAPE POINT

168

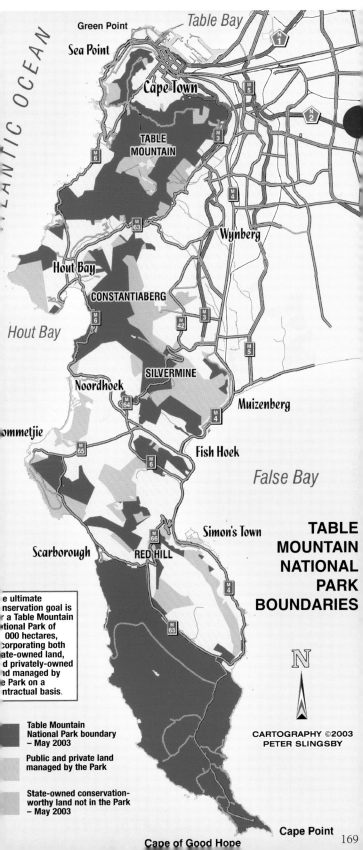

Table Bay

Green Point

Sea Point

ATLANTIC OCEAN

Cape Town

TABLE MOUNTAIN

Wynberg

Hout Bay

CONSTANTIABERG

Hout Bay

SILVERMINE

Noordhoek

Muizenberg

False Bay

Fish Hoek

Kommetjie

Scarborough

Simon's Town

RED HILL

TABLE MOUNTAIN NATIONAL PARK BOUNDARIES

The ultimate conservation goal is for a Table Mountain National Park of ...000 hectares, incorporating both state-owned land, and privately-owned ...nd managed by the Park on a contractual basis.

N

CARTOGRAPHY ©2003
PETER SLINGSBY

Table Mountain National Park boundary – May 2003

Public and private land managed by the Park

State-owned conservation-worthy land not in the Park – May 2003

Cape Point

Cape of Good Hope

169

ATLANTIC OCEAN

Green Po

Three Anchor Bay
Rocklands Bay

Graaff's
Pool

Milton Pool   Sea Po
Boat Bay
Sea Point Pavilion
Sunset Beach
Queen's Beach   Fresnaye
Sea Point
Saunders Rocks
Bantry Bay   **Bantry**
Bay
North
Paw   **LION'S HEAD**
△ 669
Clifton
Bay   ①
South   **Clifton**
Paw
Bachelor's   *Kloof Nek*
Cove
Maiden's Cove

Glen Beach
Camps Bay   **Camps**
Whale Rock   **Bay**

Bakoven Bay

Bakoven   *Pipe Track*

Klein-Koeëlbaai

Koeëlbaai

Geldkis   VICTORIA
Corridor-Ravine

Klein-Pannekoek   Witsand
OUDEKRAAL
PICNIC AREA
Groot-Pannekoek   GROOTKOP
Hottentotshuisiebaai   861

TWELVE APOSTLE

JUDAS PEAK
△ 758

Logie's Bay
Logie's Rock   Suikerbossie
Llandudno
Hout
Bay   World of   **Hout Bay**
Sunset Rocks   Nek   Birds
KLEIN-LEEUKOP   VICTORIA   Disa
Hamersteen   437   Bokkemanskloof

Sandy Bay

Oude
Schip   **Imizamo Yethu**
Rocket House   SKOORSTEENKOP
Leeugat   SUTHER PEAK   △ 540
△ 615
Die
Perd   **Hout Bay**
KARBONKELBERG
△ 653
Bakleiplaas

N

0   1km
CARTOGRAPHY ©2003
PETER SLINGSBY

Karbonkelberg Marine Reserve

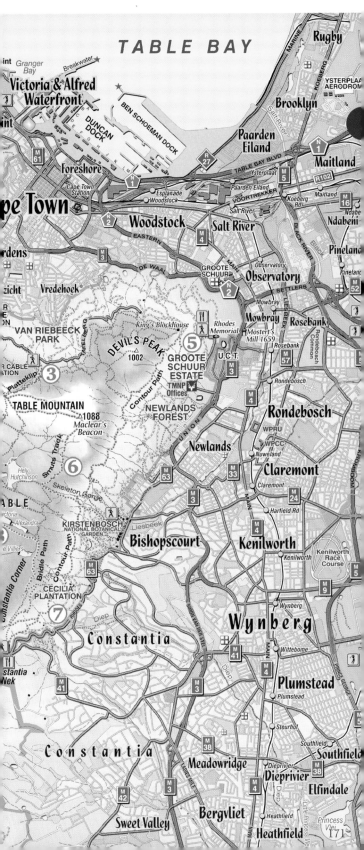

KARBONKELBERG △ 653

Hout Bay

ⓘ Hout Bay Museum

Bakleiplaas

Brako

KAPTEINSPIEK 414

Flora Bay

Old Jetty

M6

CONSTANTIA
△ 928
W

Karbonkelberg Marine Reserve

Hout Bay Harbour

York Point

THE SENTINEL △ 330

Duiker Island

Badtamboer

HOUT BAY

Blackburn Kloof

Kogel Bay

Vulcan Rock

Rondeheuwel

Vlermuisgat

M6

CHAPMAN'S PEAK

NOORDHOEK PEAK 754

10

Die Josie

M6

11

N

0   1km

CARTOGRAPHY ©2003
PETER SLINGSBY

LOWER CHAPMAN'S PEAK 547

CHAPMAN'S PEAK 593

Noordhoek

Chapman's Point

Ratelklip

Noordhoek Beach

Chapman's Bay

Occasional Tidal Pan

Chapman's Peak

NOORDHOEK

DAS

Papkuilsvlei

The Lakes

M6

Kakapo 1900

Occasional Tidal Pan

14

Klein-Slangkop Point

Sun

Masiphumelele

The Point
Bokram Beach

Long Beach

Wildevoëlvlei

Imhoff's Gift

KOMMETJIE

Kommetjie

The Island

Kommetjie Bay

KOMMETJIE

M65

Ocean View

ROOIKRANS 364

Slangkop Point

Lighthouse 1919

The Baulk

SLANGKOP 174

The Anchor

SLANGKOP

Kleinberg 127

Bokramspruit

Sweet Water

Rossouwsbank

MAIN

SANDKOP 120

M65

Maneikloof

Kle

PLATKOP △ 371

VLOOIBERG 377

Witsand

Witsand Bay

MAIN

The Island

Splash Rock
Perdebank

VARINGKOP 322

Middle Beach

Misty Cliffs

Pegram's Rock

PLATBERG △ 302

Sugarloaf Rock

Mussel Bay

Scar

172

Schuster's Bay

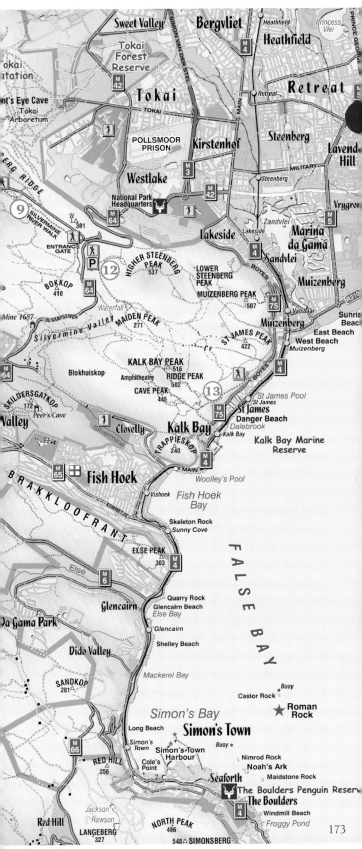

Sweet Valley
Bergvliet
Heathfield
Heathfield
Princess Vlei

Tokai Forest Reserve
okai ation
Tokai
TOKAI
Retreat
Retreat
Retreat

Int's Eye Cave
Tokai Arboretum
POLLSMOOR PRISON
Kirstenhof
Steenberg
Steenberg
Lavend Hill

ERG RIDGE
Westlake
National Park Headquarters
M3
M42
Steenberg
MILITARY
Vygron
M5

9
SILVERMINE RIVER WALK
381
W
M64
ENTRANCE GATE
12
HIGHER STEENBERG PEAK 537
LOWER STEENBERG PEAK
MUIZENBERG PEAK
Lakeside
Lakeside
Sandvlei
Zandvlei
M4
BOYES
Marina da Gama

BOKKOP 410
M64
Waterfall
OU KAAPSEWEG
Mine 1687
MAIDEN PEAK 271
Silvermine Valley
ST JAMES PEAK 422
507
M75
Valsbaai
Sunris Beac
Muizenberg
East Beach
West Beach
Muizenberg

M64
Blokhuiskop
Amphitheatre
KALK BAY PEAK 516
RIDGE PEAK 502
CAVE PEAK 445
BOYES
13
St James Pool
St James
St James
Danger Beach
Dalebrook

SKILDERSGATKOP 172
Peer's Cave
Silvermine
Clovelly
Kalk Bay
TRAPPIESKOP 240
Kalk Bay
Kalk Bay Marine Reserve
Valley

M65
Fish Hoek
M4
MAIN
Woolley's Pool
KOMMETJIE
Vishoek
Fish Hoek Bay

BRAKKLOOFRANT
Else
Skeleton Rock
Sunny Cove
ELSE PEAK 303
M4
M6
F A L S E   B A Y

Da Gama Park
Glencairn
Quarry Rock
Glencairn Beach
Else Bay
Glencairn
Shelley Beach

Dido Valley
Mackerel Bay

SANDKOP 281
Buoy
Castor Rock
★ **Roman Rock**

Simon's Bay
Simon's Town
Long Beach
Simon's Town
Buoy
Nimrod Rock
Noah's Ark
Maidstone Rock
M66
RED HILL 256
Simon's Town Harbour
Cole's Point
Seaforth
The Boulders Penguin Reserv
The Boulders
M4
Windmill Beach
Jackson Rawson
Froggy Pond

Red Hill
NORTH PEAK 486
LANGEBERG 327
548△ SIMONSBERG

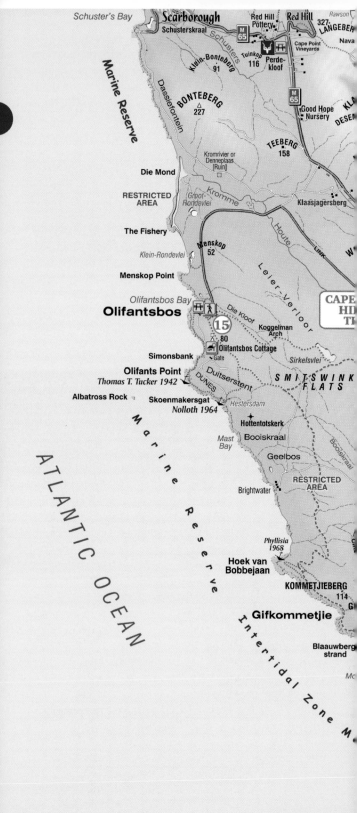

Schuster's Bay
Scarborough
Schusterskraal
Red Hill Pottery
Red Hill
327 LANGEBERG
Rawson
Nava

Schusterberg
Klein-Bonteberg 91
Tuinkop 116
Perde-kloof
Cape Point Vineyards

Dassiefontein
M 65

BONTEBERG
△ 227

Good Hope Nursery
KLA
DESEN

Kromrivier or Denneplaas [Ruin]
TEEBERG 158

Die Mond
Kromme
Klaasjagersberg

RESTRICTED AREA
Groot-Rondevlei

The Fishery
Houte
LINK

Klein-Rondevlei
Menskop 52

Menskop Point

Olifantsbos Bay
Olifantsbos
Die Kloof
Koggelman Arch
Leier-Verloor

CAPE HI T

15
△ 80
Olifantsbos Cottage
Sirkelsvlei

Simonsbank
Gate

Olifants Point
Thomas T. Tucker 1942
Duitserstent
DUNES

S M I T S W I N K F L A T S

Albatross Rock
Skoenmakersgat
Nolloth 1964
Hestersdam

Mast Bay
Hottentotskerk
Booiskraal

Booiskraal

M a r i n e

Geelbos

RESTRICTED AREA

Brightwater

A T L A N T I C

R e s e r v e

Phyllisia 1968

Hoek van Bobbejaan

KOMMETJIEBERG 114
G

O C E A N

Gifkommetjie

Intertidal Zone M

Blaauwberg strand

Mc

174

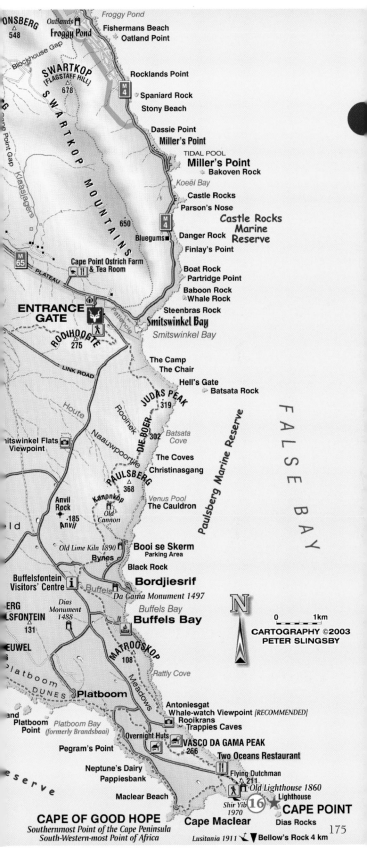

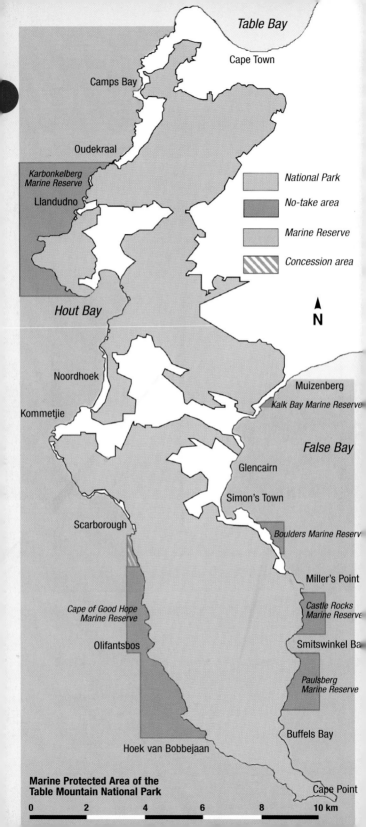

Table Bay

Cape Town

Camps Bay

Oudekraal

Karbonkelberg Marine Reserve

Llandudno

Hout Bay

	National Park
	No-take area
	Marine Reserve
	Concession area

N

Noordhoek

Muizenberg

Kalk Bay Marine Reserve

Kommetjie

False Bay

Glencairn

Simon's Town

Scarborough

Boulders Marine Reserve

Miller's Point

Cape of Good Hope Marine Reserve

Castle Rocks Marine Reserve

Olifantsbos

Smitswinkel Ba

Paulsberg Marine Reserve

Buffels Bay

Hoek van Bobbejaan

Cape Point

Marine Protected Area of the Table Mountain National Park

| 0 | 2 | 4 | 6 | 8 | 10 km |

■ Witsand beach between Scarborough and Kommetjie.

1. Zebra fish
2. Box Jellyfish
3. Loggerhead Turtle
4. Soft coral
5. Brush-tipped
   Octopus

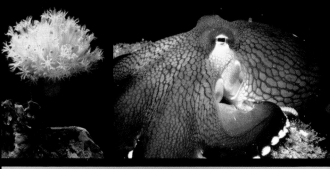

CAPE PENINSULA MARINE PROTECTED AREA

Until 2003, there were several marine reserves on the Peninsula's
coastline, but these had been proclaimed on an *ad hoc* basis over the
years to protect individual species and were largely ineffective.
Also, unmanaged harvesting and poaching had led to the
collapse of both vertebrate and invertebrate marine
resources. A new system reflecting the needs of all user
groups was therefore developed, with the Park moving
towards the proclamation of a single, 975 sq km Marine
Protected Area, managed as part the Table Mountain
National Park. The major focus in this area will be on
conservation. Fishing will still be permitted everywhere
except in a number of 'no take' zones, which will protect the
main breeding grounds of marine resources.

'The Table Mountain National Park, one of the world's premier urban national parks, provides citizens and visitors with an accessible introduction to the experience of nature. It is the Window on the Wilderness of Southern Africa, recruiting the custodians of nature who will secure the future of conservation.'
– Brett Myrdal, Park Manager

N

1:8 500 000
12mm = 100km

Kalahari Gemsbok
National Park

Richtersveld
National Park

Augrabies Falls
National Park

Namaqua
National Park

ATLANTIC
OCEAN

Tanqua Karoo
National Park

Karoo
National Pa

West Coast
National Park

Knysna Nati
Lake Are

Bontebok
National Park

Table Mountain
National Park

Wilde
Nationa

Cape Agulhas
National Park

**SOUTH AFRICAN
NATIONAL PARKS**

Vhembe/Dongola
National Park

Kruger
National Park

Marakele
National Park

Groenkloof
National Park

Golden Gate Highlands
National Park

Vaalbos
tional Park

Mountain Zebra
National Park

Addo Elephant
National Park

ikamma
nal Park

INDIAN OCEAN

Cartography ©2004
Peter Slingsby

■ USEFUL CONTACTS

EMERGENCY NUMBERS
- Central Emergency
  Services –
  From a landline:
  dial 107
  From a cellphone:
  dial 112
- Mountain Rescue:
  (021) 948-9900
- National Sea Rescue:
  (021) 449-3500
- Fires:
  (021) 535-1100
- Police Flying Squad:
  10111
- Metro Emergency &
  Ambulance:
  10177
- National Park
  24-hour emergency
  (021) 957-4700
  (021) 423-3210

POISON CENTRES
- Red Cross Children's
  Hospital
  (021) 689-5227
- Tygerberg Hospital
  (021) 931-6129

TABLE MOUNTAIN NATIONAL PARK
- Head Office
  (021) 701-8692
  fax: (021) 701-8773
  e-mail:
  capepeninsula@
  parks-sa.co.za
  On the Web:
  www.cpnp.co.za

PARK SECTION NUMBERS
- Boulders Beach
  (021) 786-2329
- Silvermine
  (021) 780-9002
- Cape Point Office
  (021) 780-9100
- Cape Point Main
  Gate (021) 780-9526
- Buffelsfontein Visitor
  Centre (Cape Point)
  (021) 780-9204

WILD CARD
086 123 4002
(021) 701-8692
fax (021) 701-8773

KAROO NATIONAL PARK
(023) 415-2828
fax (023) 415-1671
www.parks-sa.co.za/parks/Karoo/default.html

WEST COAST NATIONAL PARK
(022) 772-2144
www.parks-sa.co.za/parks/Westcoast/default.html

BONTEBOK NATIONAL PARK
(028) 514-2735
www.parks-sa.co.za/parks/Bontebok/default.html

AGULHAS NATIONAL PARK
(028) 435-6222
www.parks-sa.co.za/parks/Agulhas/default.html

RONDEVLEI NATURE RESERVE
(021) 706-2404
fax: (021) 706-2405
e-mail: rondevlei@sybaweb.co.za
On the Web:
www.rondevlei.co.za

KIRSTENBOSCH
(021) 799-8899
(021) 799-8783
www.nbi.ac.za

VISITOR INFORMATION CENTRE
- City Centre, corner
  Burg and Castle
  Streets (021) 426-4260
  Weekdays 8am – 6pm
  Sat 8.30am – 2pm
  Sun 9am – 1pm

CAPE TOWN TOURISM
(021) 423-8005
Reservations for all
National Parks can be
made here; alternatively,
(012) 343-1991

CABLEWAY
Table Mountain Aerial
Cableway Company
(021) 424-8181

FLOWER AND WHALE HOTLINE
083 123-2345
083 910-1028

RED TIDE HOTLINE
(021) 434-4457

MARINE AND COASTAL MANAGEMENT
(Information on regulations and permits for marine areas)
(021) 402-3911

MOUNTAIN CLUB
97 Hatfield Street
Cape Town
(021) 465-3412

WILDLIFE & ENVIRONMENT SOCIETY
(021) 701-1397

Friends of Lion's Head
(021) 434-6453
Friends of Silvermine
(021) 785-1477
Friends of Cape of Good
Hope (021) 785-3928
Friends of Simon's Town
Coastline (021) 786-2233
Simon's Town Flora
Conservation Group
(021) 786-1620

BOTANICAL SOCIETY
(021) 797-2090
www.botanicalsociety.org.za

CAPE BIRDING ROUTE
(021) 785-7680

KRAMATS
Cape Mazaar
Society
(021) 699-0500

MUSEUMS
see page 14.

WEATHER FORECASTS
082 162

References

Strongly Recommended:

The African Penguin. A natural history by Phil Hockey. Struik Publishers. 2001
Best Walks in the Cape Peninsula by Mike Lundy. Struik. 1999
Between Two Shores. Flora and Fauna of the Cape of Good Hope by Michael Fraser and Liz McMahon. David Philip Publishers. 1994
Discovering Indigenous Forests at Kirstenbosch by Sally Argent & Jeanette Loedolff. University of Cape Town Press. 1997
Fynbos by Richard Cowling and Dave Richardson. Photography by Colin Paterson-Jones. Fernwood Press. 1995
A Fynbos Year by Michael Fraser and Liz McMahon. David Philip Publishers. 1988
The Living Shores of Southern Africa by Margo and George Branch. C. Struik Publishers. 1981
Table Mountain. A Natural History by Anton Pauw and Steven Johnson. Fernwood Press. 1999
Table Mountain. A Natural Wonder by Glen Moll. Western Cape branch of the Wildlife and Environment Society of Southern Africa. 1987
The Table Mountain Book by Jose Burman. Human & Rousseau. 1991

Recommended:

Baboons on the Cape Peninsula. A Guide for residents and visitors by Ruth Kansky. Published by the International Fund for Animal Welfare (IFAW) and the Baboon Management Team. 2002
Cape Peninsula. South African Wild Flower Guide 3 by Mary Matham Kidd. Botanical Society of South Africa. 1983
The Essential Guide to Whales in Southern Africa by Mike Bruton. David Philip Publishers. 1998
A Field Guide to Insects of South Africa by Mike Picker, Charles Griffiths and Alan Weaving. Struik Publishers. 2002
Field Guide to Snakes and Other Reptiles of Southern Africa by Bill Branch. Struik Publishers. 1998
Frogs and Frogging in Southern Africa by Vincent Carruthers. Struik Publishers. 2001
The Invasive Alien Plant Clearing Programme 2002. Restoring the fynbos and forests to the Cape Peninsula National Park by Cape Peninsula National Park. 2002
Know Table Mountain by John Kench. Chameleon Press. 1988
Land Mammals of Southern Africa by Reay HN Smithers. Illustrations by Clare Abbott. Macmillan South Africa. 1986
Restios of the Fynbos by Els Dorrat Haaksma and H Peter Linder. Botanical Society of SA. 2000
Sasol. The Larger Illustrated Guide to Birds of Southern Africa by Ian Sinclair and Phil Hockey. Struik Publishers. 1997
Sasol. Proteas. A Field Guide to the Proteas of Southern Africa by Tony Rebelo. Fernwood Press in association with the National Botanical Institute. 2001
Two Oceans. A Guide to the Marine Life of Southern Africa by GM Branch, CL Griffiths, ML Branch and LE Beckley. David Philip. 1994
Vanishing Waters by Bryan Davies & Jenny Day. University of Cape Town Press. 1998 (South Africa's rivers, vleis, estuaries and freshwater biology)
Walking Cape Town by Gerald Rosenthal. Struik Publishers. 1999
Whale Watching in South Africa: The Southern Right Whale. by Peter B Best. Mammal Research Institute, University of Pretoria. 1995
Wild About Cape Town by Duncan Butchart. Southern Book Publishers. 1996
The Wildlife of Southern Africa. A field guide to the animals and plants of the region edited by Vincent Carruthers. Southern Book Publishers. 1997

Special thanks to:

Gary de Kock, Howard Langley, Brett Myrdal and
all the staff of the
Table Mountain National Park;
James Jackelman;
Peter Slingsby;
Anton Pauw;
June Hosford, Graham Avery & Gerald Klinghardt
of Iziko-SA Museum;
Runette Louw;
John Rogers of UCT Geology Department;
Stephen Lamb of Ukuvuka-Operation Firestop;
Callan Cohen;
Jim McLagan & Debbie McLean;
Mike Fraser & Liz McMahon;
Bruce McKenzie & Dave McDonald of the
Botanical Society of SA;
John Harrison;
Hout Bay Museum;
Joy Cobern, the Fish Hoek Valley Museum and
the Fish Hoek Art Society;
John Whitehead;
Staff of ORMS photographic dealer;
Tom Goldschmidt;
Kate Rivett-Carnac;
Janette Deacon;
Andrew Jenkins;
the staff of Paarl Print

Fonds Français pour l'Environnement Mondial &
Groupe Agence Française de Développement